THE BOYS AT TWILIGHT

GLYN MAXWELL

The Boys
at Twilight

POEMS 1990–1995

A MARINER ORIGINAL
Houghton Mifflin Company
Boston   New York
2000

Published simultaneously in Great Britain
by Bloodaxe Books Ltd.

For information about permission to reproduce
selections from this book, write to Permissions,
Houghton Mifflin Company, 215 Park Avenue South,
New York, New York 10003.

Visit our Web site: www.houghtonmifflinbooks.com.

Library of Congress Cataloging-in-Publication Data
Maxwell, Glyn, date.
The boys at twilight : poems 1990–1995
/ Glyn Maxwell.
p.   cm.
"A Mariner original."
ISBN 0-618-06414-1
I. Title.
PR6063.A869 B68   2000
821'.914—dc21   00-061325

Printed in the United States of America

QUM 10 9 8 7 6 5 4 3 2 1

for my Mother and Father

Acknowledgments

This book reprints selected poems from Glyn Maxwell's first three collections, *Tale of the Mayor's Son* (1990), *Out of the Rain* (1992), and *Rest for the Wicked* (1995), all published by Bloodaxe Books.

'The Horses' Mouths' was originally published as poems III, V, VII, and X in the sequence 'Phaeton and the Chariot of the Sun', written for *After Ovid: New Metamorphoses* (Faber, 1994). 'The Stakes' was commissioned for *The Bookworm* (BBC Television) and first published in the race guide at Newmarket. 'Yellow Plates' was written for *Klaonica: Poems for Bosnia* (Bloodaxe Books/*The Independent*, 1993).

Contents

from

TALE OF THE MAYOR'S SON

(1990)

My Turn

I have been so enchanted by the girls
who have a hunch, I have been seen

following them to the red and green
see-saws. There have been a few of them

I recognised. I have been recognised.
I have stood on the roundabout and turned.

I have swung, uselessly, not as high as them.
Then seen the parents coming, and the rain

on rusty and unmanned remaining things.
I have calculated west from the light cloud.

Cried myself dry and jumped
back on the roundabout when it had stopped.

Started it again, in the dark wet,
with my foot down, then both my feet on it.

Tale of the Mayor's Son

The Mayor's son had options. One was death,
　　and one a black and stylish trilby hat
he wore instead, when thinking this: I Love.

The town was not elaborate. The sky
　　was white collisions of no special interest
but look at the Mayor's son, at the bazaar!

'I've seen her once before...' Her name was this:
　　Elizabeth. The Mayor's son was eighteen,
his mind older than that but his mouth not.

And had no options. 'Hey, Elizabeth!'
　　I could say what was sold in the bazaar,
I could be clearer on the time of day,

I could define Elizabeth. I will:
　　Every girl you ever wanted, but
can't have 'cause I want. She was twenty-one.

'Hi, –' the name of the Mayor's son? Not the point.
　　'Let's get something together!' someone said.
'The Mayor's son out with Lisa!' someone gossiped.

The afternoon, about to be misspent,
　　stirred coffee with its three remaining fingers:
'They are sugar-crazy, they are milk-lovers,

and they won't last.' Some things about the town:
　　blue-printed in the days of brown and white
and laid down one fine evening, late July.

Musicians lived there; painters; people who
　　did murders but deliberated first;
town-councillors for other towns; widows

of chip-eating, soap-using carcasses
　　who still watch television on occasions;
ex-famous people too, well one or two,

ex-people, come to think of it; some mates
    of mine, no friends of yours, not you, not me;
a prostitute or two policemen or

a cabbage-patch doll buying a new home;
    a band of Stuart Pretenders; a fire-hose
on motorbikes, frequenting clubs and stuff;

a catholic, a protestant, a bloke;
    insurance clerks, accountants, a red horse
belonging to my cousin, and of course

the man himself. No, strike him, he just left.
    Divide the town into eleven parts,
throw ten of them away, and look at this:

They skated on the ice at the ice-rink,
    Elizabeth and a black-trilbied boy
who kept his hat on. I'd have hated that

had I seen it. I hate people who
    make such alert decisions to impress.
I'd have him on his arse. Oh good, he is.

Elizabeth, white-skirted, – no more clues –
    swooped to pick the Mayor's son off the ice,
and pterodactyl-like he shook himself.

Hat elsewhere, hat kicked on by a small bully
    and ruined by the bully's friend. Once,
that would have shelled and reddened my idea,

to see such fun. But nowadays I just
    cram it in with all the other eggs
for omelette. Skate, skate, you're crap at it,

whatever your name is, you Mayor's son.
    The Mayor's son and Elizabeth, oh my!
The middles of my afternoons in England.

Three simultaneous occurrences:
    a hump, a testimonial, a bomb.
Back to the ice-rink, just in time, we –

– There they are! Their two bicycles propped
    for vandals who'll show up in half an hour,
and off they go towards the library.

Conveniences everywhere, a town
    complete with detail, and the gardens so –
green and, and – and there! This is a poem

of love, whose hero had to urinate
    and did so, while Elizabeth began
to make a Christmas list, and left him out.

The air began to gather, pointilliste,
    and the first lamp went to a sorry pink
that wouldn't last, was a phenomenon.

They crossed roads, Beauty Gloved and the Mayor's Son,
    they made split-second choices that saved lives.
The library was all a welcome cube.

The library was full of walruses.
    Or people who resembled walruses.
Or – no. Let's say: People who would bear

comparisons with walruses, and might
    agree that was an up-to-date perception,
post-Tennyson; post-anything; French.

Outside the library, the skinhead world
    dropped litter, picked up girls, and spat, and wasn't
literate, and walruses, elsewhere,

moaned in the sea and didn't give a monkey's.
    So much for images. The library
was full of books. The books were like more books.

Some books were overdue. A man called Smith
    had borrowed Dante's *Purgatorio*
but not the other two. I had them both.

A man called Dorman had a book on trees,
    which nobody had mentioned recently
though it was ages overdue. A girl

who'd stripped the library of Sailing books
    had drowned recently, and was so slow
to answer warnings that they'd phoned her up

to ask politely for their library books.
    A dictionary had gone missing too
but the Mayor's son had other things in mind!

How do we know? We don't, but he had options,
    and watched Elizabeth selecting books
on Archaeology, and calling them

'Unusually specific.' The Mayor's boy
    nodded his head of ordinary hair
and felt Love making soup with the utensils

he generally called his heart and soul.
    'Well this is it,' she said, 'but it's too short.'
The sky was mauve, no other colour, mauve –

the walruses, the ice-skaters, the books!
    The Mayor himself was coming home to dinner,
and I was splitting up with Alison.

I think it was that day, about half-six.
    The bully, meanwhile, read about a bike
and mentioned it to his belaboured dad

as a potential Christmas present. I –
    sometimes I hope he gets it, sometimes I
devoutly hope it kills him. Anyway,

'The Library is closing now.' The Mayor
    expected his son home. Elizabeth
expected that as well, didn't expect

what happened next as they waited for the cars
    to lose their nerve and stop. He put his hand
behind the head of this Elizabeth

and bruised her with a kiss, a mad one! He
    receded and she reappeared, a girl
with somebody to marry, and not him,

her mouth politicised indignity,
    her eyes becoming tyrants, après-coup:
'How dare you?' What a question. How dare *you*?

Because we don't know what – because we do –
    Irrelevant! Elizabeth was off.
The traffic-lights were either green or red –

I don't see amber. Look at the Mayor's son,
    no girl, no hat, under the sodium-
lamps of his home town. (Elizabeth

was born here too. Actually, so was I,
    but Alison moved here in '83.)
Change, traffic-lights! Go, hatchbacks of the time,

the buses, and the other cars! Next year
    the Mayor – who now eats fillets with his wife
and son, and fills a second glass with Soave

and tells a joke, and the son laughs – the Mayor
    will be deposed next year: his son will choose
a university, *it* will say no

to him but take Elizabeth, for Maths
    not Archaeology, and Alison
will suddenly, one day, in a Maths class,

befriend Elizabeth, and find that their
    acquaintances are mutual, like me
and the Mayor's son, and in a stand-up bar

all evening they'll be there. Meanwhile the books
    will pile up in my world, and someone's hat
will find its way to me and I will wear it.

Drive to the Seashore

We passed, free citizens, between the gloves
of dark and costly cities, and our eyes
bewildered us with factories. We talked.

Of what? Of the bright dead in the old days,
often of them. Of the great coal-towns, coked
to death with scruffy accents. Of the leaves

whirled to shit again. Of the strikers sacked
and picking out a turkey with their wives.
Of boys crawling downstairs: we talked of those

but did this: drove to where the violet waves
push from the dark, light up, lash out to seize
their opposites, and curse to no effect.

Flood Before and After

It reeled across the North, to the extent
that even Northerners said 'This is North!'
and what would you have said, to see a sky

threatening the children with great change?
Extraordinary clouds! Spectaculars!
There was the Dimden family, in their barn.

And long, quite vertical rain, the three horizons
hunched, different formulations, browns
and oranges. Then the unlucky Greens

running with their sons to find their sons.
The scarecrow and the crow, they did okay,
getting dark together, but unfrightened.

Fists of clouds! Genii of glamour!
Not to mention thunders, not again!
There stand the Dimdens, safe for once and sad.

The Greens have found their sons! Now for their daughters.
But out goes the lightning, giant's fork
into a mound of chilli, steaming there

and where's it gone? Into the open mouth,
barn and all, flavours and seasonings!
Cuddle in the rain, old favourites.

There goes a Noah, borrowing a plank.
A little slow to move, we thought. It ends
with tangles, the new rivers, and the sunshine

formally requesting a rainbow. Granted.
The creaking and excusing back to work.
A valuable man was lost in it.

That was in the paper, with the picture.
All the Northern correspondents went
reading to the telephones, all cold,

which brought the dry onlookers from the South,
gaspers, whistlers, an ambassador
and leading lights to mingle with the hurt.

The clouds were diplomats of the same kind,
edging over to exonerate
and praise. And then the royal son arrived,

helicoptered down on a flat field,
glancing up at the sky through the whuz of blades,
attending to the worried with a joke.

Hell, I don't know what – we were all cold.
The landscape looked an archipelago.
The Dimdens finally twigged, the Greens were found

beating the Blooms at rummy, in a cave.
All were interviewed and had lost all.
All saluted when the helicopter rose.

Only some came up the knoll with us
to check our options. Only two of those
saw, as I did, Noah's tiny boat

scarcely moving on the edge of sight
below the line, and only I'd admit
the crow and the scarecrow were rowing it.

The Albatross Revolution

I

The Residence was coddled by the light
of albatrosses, many of them silent.

The summerhouse had had a green door then,
which banged and banged and shut, and the relevant

daughters of their Highnesses were to be seen
nowhere – probably putting on a play

or, at that flashpoint of the century,
heading somewhere new, reluctantly.

II

The albatrosses having flown inland,
the green door flew open. The daughters and

the friends they had were two groups that were not
there, and starlings were a small group that was,

though not for long. The lawn was wide and cold
with all these new commotions, and the sea

licked at the bony ankles of the cliff
as if it was their Highnesses. It rained.

III

Somebody laughed hysterically when
the full whiteness of the Residence

exposed itself to all – the random all
who shoved each other out of the forest now.

The starlings jabbed in the orangery.
The albatrosses did something different

elsewhere, the details quite available.
There was some sour cream in the Residence.

IV

There were some bottles in the sea. The cliff
had stood ten centuries of them, and would,

to be honest, stand twenty centuries more.
Men climbed the chimneys of the Residence

even as podgy womenfolk exchanged
recipes involving cheese and sour cream.

And they flew flags, the men. And starling crap
made constellations on the cold wide lawn.

V

It rained. Whatever the flag meant, it sulked
or, at that flashpoint of the afternoon,

resulted in all sorts of things. The cream
was put to its sour use. The Residence

was multi-purpose, snaps of albatrosses
hung all about. The air grew dark and green

as uniforms, and, catapulting out
of a high window, the Albatross-Man.

Mandate on an Eighth of May

There came a mandate for a street-parade.
On Optington Lane, which my good friend S
called Pessington for obvious reasons.

And I called it neither, not living there.
There came a mandate for a street-parade
on George the Eighth of May, and Mrs Bain

rose to the occasion, vase in hand,
to celebrate the celebration of
the very good things that were happening

all over Optington, which my partner J
did not approve of, and she kissed me hard.
Which was a different good thing happening,

which would have happened anyway, without
the flags and ticker-tape and elderly
and large endorsers of the government.

Whose victory was Optington Lane's
victory! By which I mean the sun
was truly out and the sky truly blue –

down in that shine the wine was sipped, the nine
kinds of sandwiches were sampled, Mrs
Bain practised her speech on herself, Mrs

Applechooser waited for a sign from
the neighbour, whom she loved, and Dr Pools
strolled between the tables with his beard.

When I say street-parade I mean street-party.
That nothing moved in step, neither towards
St Palmer's Church nor down to the Drill Hall

but gathered round about seventy tables
(not counting chairs) and each covered in white
and, as Major Crammer put it, 'Eats'.

My correspondent F put it like this:
'If you can't beat 'em, wait until they croak.
Then you can laugh at them.' My partner J

isn't keen on that, and nor am I.
'Better to laugh at them and drink their wine,'
she said, and kissed me hard, and drank my wine.

All of which explains why she and I
(the love between which can't be that. Explained,
I mean) stood our green ground among the guests

although we didn't live there, or agree.
On certain things – fashion, the occult, God –
not even with each other. 'I agree,'

Miss Partofit was overheard to say
to Dr Pools and the new neighbour's wife,
'This is a moral victory for us.'

'Sweeping up the tide,' said Mr Bain.
'Making the only choice,' agreed the wife.
'Hanging is too good,' ventured a tall

pillar of the local cricket club.
My partner J was circling the tables,
mixing up the wines to make rosés,

and then swapping addresses with an old
donor who said 'Ah, your eyes are brown...'
To which she answered, 'Take this number down.'

And I confined myself to making notes
and placing sandwiches in people's bags.
And writing to a mentor, W,

to say 'We are both well, the world and I.
J has made it what it could be worth.
F reports on it, and S stays sad.

And I would call it Optington, despite
the never-ending news from Whitepool Town
and Roxeter, the illnesses and blame,

the poverty and closures north of here
and west of here and east, despite the rumours
surrounding what occurred at Linsaydown,

despite the hundred dead off the white coast.
Despite the thousand missing now in Thaza.
Despite the million said to have been seen

in Ghad, and the one running after them.
And the long line between Black and Notblack.
And the Presidents waving inside their skins.

Despite the day or night the telephone brings
the cut, and I sit down and need a hand
and brandies, I will call it Optington

and when the jolly sights of Optington Lane's
big big day have been cleared away and swept,
and the flags hanging in the elms look wrong,

and Mrs Bain is very much alone,
and it is really night, I will tell you, you
W who knows it anyway:

we never stole from Optington. My J
knew too much to do that. We never told
a single fat and sipping soul that all

their celebrations made us want to cry
for them. We stole away, remembered as
two strangers who belonged to someone else.'

We did, and then we drank our own concoction
on George the Eighth of May in Optington.
Watching the motorway, watching the cars

of strangers. Watching the stars, or two of them.
It had got cloudy. 'It hurts,' one of us said.
'It hurts, and then it stops,' the other said.

Together, on the bridge, in Optington
on Earth – a real place, not one of my
inventions – we were quiet, it was late:

see us. Remember us. Remember the date.

The Pursuit

Running through woods he came to the wrong wood,
the round wood. And he stopped there like a man
would in a sudden temple, and his own blood beat
on the cocked side, his hurt side, his red portside.

Running through trees like a deer, victimised,
a sprinter, of a minority, he passed
on into blacker greens and deep betweens,
lost to sight. We shrugged the Home County shrug.

'Running?' muttered those who report and wait:
'quickly?' added by them with a hunch and pencil:
'and with a scared look?' mentioned by the cadets:
'away?' as was firmly noted by those who are here,

he was seen. The relevant people looked for him,
I know, because their vans were parked on the rim
of the right wood, and they took their torches with them,
and left their maps and their furry animals hanging.

'Running, quickly, away, with a scared look?
Escaping.' The constructed xeroxed faces
appeared on walls from here to the uncrossable
M110, and it was said

the outer elms came back to life when the wire
linked them, to politely counsel 'Don't',
and in the ring of fire the rare and common,
darting, hopping, slithering, trudging, dragging

towards life-leasing coldness, from the smoke,
met in the heart of the wood and stared and were doomed.
It was said in the crackle and crack the stars went out.
The birds alone took life and the news away.

In the dry filth of the aftermath the drivers
found belongings, bagged and took them and waited.
Then radioed superiors on the rim.
But he ran elsewhere, though a red X was him.

Mild Citizen

Sunday is wringing its discoloured hands.
The elms are rinsed of light and greenness, birds
shit and circle over these charlatans
who haggle in the field. I do my work,
        scotching the short words
I really want, the ragged and berserk,
in favour of a point of view. I lean
into the vertical, out of the murk
which pulls and changes what it didn't say
        and didn't know, but mean,
and I'm ready. Ever younger people play
there or near, as the adult town of men
fills up with us, and yellow yesterday
in its sheets, smells. When it gets late
        I walk, mild citizen
of what's suggested, what's appropriate
because it saves my neck. Only, again,
I see the pale, shock-headed Delegate
emerging from the Chamber, and I hear
        the moaning on the lane,
where the mild citizens keep moving, where
empty musicians play in endless rain.

The High Achievers

Educated in the Humanities,
they headed for the City, their beliefs
implicit in the eyes and arteries
of each, and their sincerity displayed
in notes, in smiles, in sheaves
of decimal etcetera. Made,
they counted themselves free. Those were the hours
of self-belief, and the slow accolade
of pieces clattering into a well.
And then the shrug of powers,
and the millions glutted where they fell
toadstooling into culture. Who knows when
they made their killings during that hot spell:
flies or policemen? An infinity
of animals began
to thrive especially, as when the dull sea,
sick with its fish, was turning them to men.

Wasp

We were all strained with the food when look, a wasp
was and saw what it smelt on our white table
that damnably good summer: it saw the best

thing for now. The bee was near but wiser,
off engineering better from her own
mauve flowers in a basket off the hot wall:

she didn't want what we had wanted and had,
our spoils and fluids. The wasp rose out and passed
from salad to salad, amazed I suppose with how many

there were to approach and envisage. You,
suddenly poised, with a weapon
lightly awaiting, waited. And when I looked

you all had coshes and swatters and so did I.
The nasty little guy
chose to buzz our heads and would die because

of what it wanted and was.
We enjoyed that animal pause in our long lunch,
armed, mates in sweat and our local luck.

We got it. Who got it? I got it,
and dissuaded the boys from keeping it
frizzing in a jar forever and ever. I crushed it.

Well, I thought, as the bee moved off to tell –
but heavily, bored with its maddening cousins – well:
don't fuck with us, little guys. We're mad as hell.

The End of the Weekend

The chairs were folded up when the light was,
mid-Sunday afternoon; the poplar trees

prepared to bend, and bent, and stood again
behind these disappointed people, ten

assorted family-members, girls and blokes
spending the day as uncles, sisters, folks,

and now, with the bad summer in its shed,
ten private citizens, reflecting, sad,

the family a name, the drinks all drunk
before predicted rain. No one to thank

now, and the two red cars a mile along
the wide woodside road. No one said nothing

as the group walked, except the husband who,
in finally admitting that he knew,

omitted to tell anyone, except,
later, his youngest, who was tired, had slept,

and wouldn't carry anything. Her brother,
two steps, two years ahead, wouldn't either,

and the slim eldest sister, who was tired
of a new boyfriend she had long desired,

was carrying the hamper. The first fork
of lightning shot, split, lit up the whole park!

In what followed, the mother of the three
said she'd been right. No one could disagree.

The thunder came and was a friend to all
who wanted this late failure dark and full,

an excuse for hot toast later, and then
much much later, to be remembered-when.

Then the half-mile mark came, and with it more
of the same slanting unrelenting pour.

The quiet husband crossed the road (this side
had only a grass verge, no paving.) Odd,

how very slowly and diagonally,
gradually, the rest of his family

did the same thing, waiting for this green truck
to screech along, and slow, as if to look

at the divided, drenched and carrying
people, and then to wrench off, rattling.

At last the move was made. This family
had the name Anderson. No tragedy

had struck. In general, they were content.
They never tried to be a thing they weren't,

and what they were, they didn't think was best
or most important. They belonged and fussed

and voted when they would. The other five,
the yet-unnoted, had the name of Love

(no really) – Mrs Love (*née* Black) was Mrs
Anderson's (*née* Black's) sister, and this is

her, holding the dark blankets, her coat
as dark, in the at long last slackening wet.

'Nearly there,' and that was Mr Love,
needlessly consoling, soaked enough

to tell the story, Monday, at the site.
And their one son behind them, fairly bright

and cracking jokes at somebody's expense,
somebody dead now, taking no offence.

That's eight. There was an older Mr Love,
leading from the front, and his new wife

gamely alongside, cheering up the kids.
Another blink of lightning, and the hoods

of dwarfs along the roadside, counting up:
'One, elephant, Two, elephant, Three –' (CLAP!)

cruel over a different town, not theirs.
That's ten. That's all of them. They reached the cars

and as the rain ended, and the green light
air was breathed – it was still not all that late –

they towered themselves in, and some of them
were unseen. None of them was clear. A dim

thunder I could hear, preceded by no
lightning, nothing – no I don't think so –

they drove away. One drove away, then two,
and there was nothing. What those people do

now is everything. I know that now.
Don't tell me different. What they do, how,

under the rains of these bad summers, that
is all that's going to change, going to get

things better, fairer, cured, allowed to grow
on the great field, in the great shops tomorrow

filled with the many selves. And in new rain
the neither-here-nor-there but with a plan

were home by now, I guess, the TV on,
the kettle hushed and boiling, the day gone,

the house perhaps all light. But I don't know,
and when you tell me things you think you know,

don't tell me what they look like, how they sound.
Tell me what kind they are, and how kind.

A Whitsun

One of the very first
reasons for what
they would term their love
would have been the green wet
of a late afternoon of
truancy, cloudburst.

Having run they'd breathe
and wonder whether
the hoped and unhoped-for
would stumble together
now, unlooked for
but felt beneath.

And kitchen chairs scrape
an obvious answer
loudly together:
an in-joke, a glance, a
biscuit, another,
a favourite tape

and their quiet eyes
to the window, where
the fostering things –
the rain in the air,
the remembered songs,
the light – would uprise

over the town in their
guaranteeing it.
Meanwhile the adamant
aftermath of what
was a kiss – which meant
the beginning for her –

meant it to him:
a phoning October,
a pairing for shelter
and diaries. Neither
would suffer that winter
or forget that time

but this was the difference,
among the very first
subjects they talked of
and almost the last:
she'd never tire of
hot sun – his preference

was the lucky white breath
of a freezing day,
with a pub, its gleam,
its fire. Anyway,
Whitsun came
with the patterned cloth

creased on the grass
and the ambushing first
wasps, and their moods
outstretched and burst –
they spoke at odds.
The dispersing class

dispersed them, yawning,
he to his hayfever,
she to her calm
and turned head sleeping
on a lotioned arm
any brilliant morning.

Just Like Us

It will have to be sunny. It can rain only
when the very plot turns on pain and postponement,
the occasional funeral. Otherwise perfect.

It will have to be happy, at least eventually
though never-ending and never exactly.
Somebody must, at the long-last party,

veer to the side to remember, to focus.
All will always rise to a crisis,
meet to be shot for a magazine Christmas.

It will also be moral: mischief will prosper
on Monday and Thursday and seem successful
but Friday's the truth, apology, whispered

love or secret or utter forgiveness.
It will have to be us, white and faulty,
going about what we go about. Its

dark minorities will *be* minorities,
tiny, noble and gentle, minor
characters in more offbeat stories.

Its favourite couple will appear in our towns,
giving and smiling. Their tune will be known
by all from the lonely to the very young

and whistled and sung. It will all be repeated
once. Its stars will rise and leave,
escaping children, not in love,

and gleam for a while on the walls of girls,
of sarcastic students beyond their joke,
of some old dreadful unhappy bloke.

It will have to be sunny, so these can marry,
so these can gossip and this forgive
and happily live, so if one should die

in this, the tear that lies in the credible
English eyes will be sweet, and smart
and be real as blood in the large blue heart

that beats as the credits rise, and the rain
falls to England. You will have to wait
for the sunny, the happy, the wed, the white. In

the mean time this and the garden wet
for the real, who left, or can't forget,
or never meant, or never met.

Tale of a Chocolate Egg

I

The advertising of the chocolate egg
began that day. The slogan was so short
it was the chocolate egg and only that.

The chocolate egg alone on a silk surround.
A little cream-filled general in bed
was what I thought of when I saw it, but

I hadn't seen it yet, and play no part.
The advertising was quite marvellous.
I even saw a lad discard his Mars

in open-mouthing awe at the vast ad.
It was enormous, a whole building's wall!
The walls of a whole block! The chocolate egg

alone in bed, its slogan, as I said,
itself. Look, like this: *O*. But obviously
magnified a million more times.

You couldn't see its centre, it was whole
and flawless, like a real egg. It *was*
a real egg, or representation of

a real egg, or a real chocolate egg.
You couldn't see what came inside it, but,
you could guess it would delight and ooze.

It would, it would be yellow with some white,
a real egg, as we observed earlier.
And children gathered, hoping, under it.

II

Irrelevant and independent, warm
in recently-washed sheets, the brown-haired bloke
awoke. He was both hungry and hungover:

he'd been peripheral at an all-niter.
The last thing he remembered was the blonde
asking him not to dance. There'd been a game

in which one told the truth. He'd told a lie
and nobody had been surprised. The blonde
had somehow won. That was a different blonde.

The brown-haired bloke felt dizzy at the window,
a first-floor window, over the east of town.
A massive dirty town. London, in fact.

He saw the houses of about a half
million. He lived on a small hill.
He saw a dozen people on the streets.

'All those people...' sighed the boy whose hair
was the most ordinary possible.
Brown, neat when combed, a normal length,

not all that clean. 'People without names...'
he postulated, wrongly, falling back
across the bed, with nothing else to say.

He checked his Rockwatch. It was Saturday.
He stretched his arms, or sang, or scratched his legs.
Then thought of breakfast. Bacon, maybe eggs.

III

In the last corner of the last corner shop
there served an Indian girl. She watched the door.
(Her parents were out back, watching the back door

for more deliveries.) A skinhead came.
'Twenny B'n'H, a pack o'reds,
some baccy an' a Sun, sweet'art,' he said,

chewing, sniffing, glancing at the goods.
The Indian girl sold them, and he paid,
and, as he made to leave, he had a thought.

It was a short and vital thought. It came
sharply to his mind, and it got said.
'Also, sweet'art. I'll have a chocko egg.'

He had it. There were hundreds on the streets!
(People) it was Saturday, the sky
was dry, allowing white, this was a time

of celebration in the banks and pubs:
they'd just confirmed the four-percent decline
in non-violent crime, and wedding bells

had sounded in the new soap, *Cul-de-Sac*!
Flinzi's pic was everywhere from ELLE
to MLLE, via the *Sunday Times*,

and in the clean hands of the brown-haired bloke
though he just read it for the horoscope.
It said he would be lucky. He looked up.

IV

The sun was on its way from I to J,
as it were, way up there, London's own.
The skinhead sat down by the marketplace

and coughed and smoked, and read his newspaper.
He turned a page and 'Cor!' he said aloud,
then turning to the middle, a young man,

he carried on with being unaware
of being watched by constables and there,
in the sunshine, his ex-girlfriend, Clare.

And in his bag his chocolate purchase warmed.
A family nearby had seen the ad,
the egg, and they began admiring it.

The children were young children, and, as if
they'd just been told that, started to complain:
'I want one.' 'I want two.' 'We want two

each.' The egg itself, its sun-gloss brown
underlining its fine quality,
luxuriated silkily, and sold

– to the family, standing in the last
corner shop, and buying 'Six eggs, please.'
The Indian girl was reaching for the best

fresh farm produce, when a small voice said:
'Not those white ones, Daddy, we want these!'
They got them. And the shop-girl watched them leave.

V

Down in the Dwelling of the Brown-Haired Bloke
the brown-haired bloke was hungry. In his fridge,
cool absences and gaps made him a fool:

no milk, no bread. At least not in his section.
Lindsay's shelf had bacon, milk and juice,
croissants, all necessary breakfast things,

while Oliver's, of course, was mainly beer
and the odd onion bhaji. As for his,
pâté and a lemon, and a sole

hopeful, cracked, and all-hope-shattering egg.
He couldn't nick. He went unbreakfasted
in a quiet room of feasible breakfasts.

There was a silver lining. There were some
seventy-five teabags he could use.
He used one, took it black, and used the lemon.

'I'm having lemon tea,' he said, truly.
'It's no bad thing sometimes to go hungry.'
'Bollocks,' said his stomach, a young Tory.

He re-opened his magazine. So many
adverts nowadays, hardly a page
of honest information, he was thinking,

turning the pages. Then he heard a sound
upstairs, thought something of it, then sat back.
Gave a sigh, decided to go out.

VI

It ought to have been gathered: it was hot.
The children's eggs were softening or gone
and the parents? merely coping, as they'd done

a thousand times before. More than that.
The last corner shop was cool, though, all
the goods were cool and sound, the sell-by dates

were up ahead – perilous sell-by dates!
No one underestimates them now,
not since the old lady died in Glossop.

The owner of the shop, the girl's father,
was puzzled. He was in the shop himself:
'These eggs, so very popular...' he mused.

His daughter humbly nodded: 'All this morning,
everyone.' 'I cannot understand,'
the owner said. (He'd try one, later on,

throw most of it away, and remain puzzled.
She, however, nodding now, in fact
had eaten one, and hidden one.) They shrugged.

The sun reached *N*, then it was afternoon.
The skinhead rose and recognised the head
of Clare, his ex, her hair extremely red,

her bangled hands haggling over bangles.
'Oi, sweet'art!' he shouted in the sun.
Not nobody's sweetheart, she carried on.

VII

And out into the day ambled the one
unbreakfasted and eager citizen
yet to see what new thing had been done.

The brown-haired bloke saw children seeing it,
he saw their parent(s) seeing it and groaning,
he saw hot drivers bored and interested.

Then he saw it. A vast advertisement
for chocolate eggs. It was a chocolate egg,
or paper reproduction, but enormous.

There was no slogan. That did strike him then –
the sheer nerve, the worthless new idea!
Filling up that gap on that old building!

He'd stopped by now, the bloke. He also thought
it did resemble something not an egg.
Something lazing in a rich man's bed,

something bald and powerful, perhaps
a general. He scoffed at it, and walked
(thinking of the immorality,

40

the trivial creativity, the waste!)
straight into the skinhead. 'Fuckin'ell!
Watch it, mate… Oi, sweet'art, wait for me!'

The hungry bloke, forgotten, rubbed his head.
Blinked in the exacting sunlight, stood
pondering in his rough neighbourhood.

VIII

For he was the next customer. His feet
were inches from the nearest corner shop.
He looked relieved, and jangled through the door.

The door jingled behind him. He was in
and choosing bacon, bread, some apple juice
if possible, and being shown it was:

the Indian girl was pleased to see his hair.
In the dark behind her loomed her father,
worriedly stocktaking in the corner.

The brown-haired bloke got ready with his choices:
bacon, bread, milk, apple juice. He checked
a scribbled list, and mentioned eggs aloud.

The father froze. The girl looked in the box
marked CHOCOLATE EGGS, and saw how few there were.
Four: there'd been a run. She touched the box.

'God, not those things,' chuckled the customer,
always right, and looking in the box,
'The ones that come from farmers!' He bought six.

A satisfying customer, he left,
mulling over possibilities:
a bacon sandwich, poach the eggs perhaps.

Tea with milk, but in which cup? The brown?
Yes, call it a brunch. The bloke looked up.
Clouding over now. 'In the brown cup.'

IX

The afternoon, some three hours after noon,
not unlike the marketplace, began
to let in gaps and sighs of weariness.

Women stretched, men bent down to lift.
Karen, Clare, and Karen from the hat-stall
made their way towards a corner shop,

via the long pavement over which
the cloud-darkened egg presided, big.
They chatted as girls do, as some girls do,

they jingled in, acknowledged by the owner,
who'd let his daughter out to buy the fish.
They made a lot of noise, and what they bought

is not important. What they didn't, is:
a chocolate egg. They bought three, certainly,
but left a single one. Just 30p!

You'd think they'd go the whole hog, wouldn't you?
Instead they left, chatting as some girls do.
The door jangled behind them. In the shop,

a good man's consternation at supply
almost dry, demand still running high:
he glared at the chocolate egg... But outside, this:

'Sweet'art, wait for me! I wanna talk!'
The skinhead chased his ex down Bootlace Street.
The Karens shrieked, began to overeat.

X

Digesting on his own, in a dull room,
checking on the fixtures, switching on
the tiny colour television, seeing

various ridiculous programmes, each
greeted with a groan and some attention,
some twenty seconds till another change,

from all the matches after half-an-hour
strangely at 0–0, (on ORACLE)
to tribesmen fishing things on Channel 4,

to endless steeplechasing in the rain
at Haydock Park and Doncaster and a Welshman
coming sixty-fourth in a downpour,

to that same and increasingly bizarre
black-and-white from 1944,
in which the Colonel opens the wrong door

and reads the latest scores – to CEEFAX now,
where most games were 1 – 1, and the good news
on the news-sheet, 102, the crash,

was that the firemen, ambulancemen, guardsmen,
policemen, passers-by, ringmasters, kids,
backwoodsmen, poets, acrobats, and thieves

had done a marvellous job, and the death-toll
was falling rapidly, and Heads of State
were representing us by being there

XI

a while after the dying, – and changing back
to final betting on the 4.15,
the Colonel saying 'I don't know what you mean!'

the tribesmen being interviewed, the match
at Alloa abandoned, and the race
won convincingly by seven Kenyans,

and lunch's rumble settled, the sound upstairs
of Oliver, inching towards the shower,
and all our Saturdays the usual, he,

the brown-haired bloke, he – anyway, he sighed.
'Rubbish,' he said, switched to another side
he didn't know existed. It was new.

Its name was STAR, (Lindsay must've
fixed it up, a dish outside?) it showed
seven different programmes: at that instant

Cul-de-Sac was on, an episode
the brown-haired bloke had never seen, in which
Flinzi, the success-story, was sad.

She wasn't getting on with her real dad.
The dad she had was smiling just behind her.
She cried all the way to the commercials.

The bloke was laughing 'Ha! It's rubbish! Ha!'
Rather loudly, everything else was quiet.
Then came this particular commercial.

XII

o. A brown *o*, starting rather small.
(Hell, you know what's coming, but he didn't.)
A bigger, browner, chocolatier *O*

impossible to demonstrate, but there
on its silk background lay the one
unannotated, unexplained, unsold

egg of earlier. Still there was no slogan.
There *was* music, either by Johnny Cash,
the Beatles or the Everlys, whoever,

but not a word was spoken. By the end,
by the thirtieth second, the whole screen
was brown and cream-filled. Then, on white, the words

CUL-DE-SAC. For rather a long time.
Then Shane accusing Laurel, Laurel hurt,
Stacy curious, Roger on the prowl,

and Flinzi bravely smiling through. Through what?
The television wasn't on. These things
occurred elsewhere and who knows where? The room

was empty, and the front door lightly shut.
Nothing happened here, unless you count
Oliver's bedraggledly appearing,

eating Lindsay's bacon, someone's eggs,
someone's croissant, settling down to watch
the end of *Cul-de-Sac*. Someone got shot.

XIII

'Just the one,' the bloke was thinking, 'Just
to try, it's bound to be disgusting, just
to experience a culinary low…'

He crossed at the pedestrian crossing,
ahead of the pedestrians, it seemed
to him they heard him, censured him for thinking

'culinary' – probably they'd laugh
to see him clip the kerb! Serve 'im right!
they'd think – he thought, he did, and then they did:

'Enjoy yer trip?' laughed someone in a fez.
'But is it hunger?' was a later thought,
while walking by the finished marketplace,

'or merely greed?' 'It's greed,' said half of him,
the upper half; 'It's hunger,' went the rest,
all accomplished liars there, but charmers.

There was the advertisement, the hoarding!
A great, swollen full-stop on his hopes
of backing out, and the silk made it worse:

The bloke was going to eat the chocolate egg!
There it was, in brown-and-purple! Big!
There was the corner shop! In which he'd even

said he didn't want to, and meant it!
What would they think of him – Avid, pale,
returning, with a brown look in his eye?

XIV
'In the extraordinary, implausible
but nonetheless respected – if bizarre –
event of your not being totally

and utterly, completely, creamily,
dreamily, creme-fondant centrally
satisfied, delighted, nay, amazed,

converted, charmed and spellbound by our product,
– strange, somewhat perverse as such dissent
may seem to decent, civilised consumers –

you may of course tell us precisely what
has worried you, disturbed you in your great
cloud-cadbury-land of culinary nous,

and even tell us where you deigned to purchase
such unpleasing fare, and roughly when
you thought you'd stretch to 30p for this

Cadillac of Chocolates – thank you so much! –
we'd obviously bend arse over tit
accommodating you, mighty one:

just tell us who could do with some cheap chocs,
and where they live. We'll send our Family Box.'
'Nutrition Information. Every egg

contains 8g Fat, 1.7 Protein,
Carbohydrate 26.5.'
ROLAND RAT SAYS KEEP YOUR COUNTRY CLEAN.

XV

The brown-haired bloke was at the door. He had
a hot pound coin in his hand, his face
expressed a wish to be expressionless,

and he was in the shop. The aisles were narrow,
the place was empty, but for the quiet mother
gazing past the bloke at the canned soups,

then he was at the counter. There was a box,
being somewhat profligate with the facts:
CHOCOLATE EGGS – a bald untruthful plural.

The bloke observed the egg in all its smallness.
Its wrapper was all shiny reds and golds,
unlike the brazen nude advertisement –

which hadn't been a factor, he assured
his upper house of cerebral detractors,
all whistling him to pay his stupid coin

and live with it. He opened his whole mouth
as someone charged into the shop, the door
jingling apologetically behind –

'Gimme a half o''Teachers, sweet'art! Oi,
you again! Outta me way, I'm first!
An' I'll 'ave that chocko egg an'all, sweet'art!

Me fuckin' sweet'art's buggered off, sweet'art!
'ere – 'ave a fiver, that'll do it. Oi,
watch it, matey! Ta-ra, Gunga Din!'

XVI

He jangled out. The daughter jingled in,
without the fish, but telling her mother why
in Urdu. As for the next customer,

he bought TIME, with the planet on its front.
Then he left, now harrowingly hungry.
A sad agreement of his bickering halves.

The shopkeepers had looked at him strangely.
Then chattered in their language. The girl moved
over to the counter, where the box

boasting CHOCOLATE EGGS was a brown lie.
She picked it up and said some more. Her mother
made a sign of resignation, almost

philosophical, then turned away,
back into the rooms behind, talking.
The daughter heard the radio go on,

heard of the shock-result in Liverpool,
the muddy draw in Middlesbrough, the old
world-record broken by a man called Ngu,

the amazing binding packs of the All-Blacks
and gallant British losses everywhere.
And she didn't understand, and didn't care.

The day's last customers were from the States.
They were lost. 'We're looking for... the East?'
'You are here,' the Indian told them. They weren't pleased.

XVII

Safe in the Dog and Barrow, Clare the Ex-
Girlfriend of the Skinhead sipped her half
and gained the weight she'd lost escaping him.

Karen, Karen from the hat-stall, Wayne,
Bruno, Debs and Shaz from the Arndale
began three conversations, one on clothes,

one on that 1–1 draw at Anfield, one
on that same skinhead standing by the door
watching them, filling his beer-glass

with shots of Teachers whisky. 'Well I'm thirsty,'
he told the nearest codger, who was deaf
and hadn't asked. It must have been 'round six.

It was just then the Americans came in,
ordering what couldn't be provided.
Angry that it couldn't be provided.

'We'll sort 'im out,' said Wayne, at the round table.
'If he comes near you –' Bruno said. 'He will,'
said Karen from the hat-stall, quite excited:

'He did this afternoon! She had to peg it!'
'Yeah,' said Clare, 'No fanks to you.' 'What for?'
the blonder Karen shrieked: 'He ain't *our* boyfriend!'

Not no one's boyfriend, overhearing all,
the skinhead scratched his head and made a plan.
'I'll sort 'er out,' he told a passing man.

XVIII

A cool and clouded dusk was coming on.
The sun had gone to pieces long before,
and one or two had felt drops on the wind.

The brown-haired bloke had walked a half-mile west
in search of other corner shops. He'd passed
burger-houses, hair-salons, bookies,

estate agents, and video rental shops,
but nothing quite like what he needed. Or,
wanted. He was past the needing stage,

really he was just walking a new way,
he didn't know the area at all.
He wanted to get something from today.

But most things were closed, and he began,
by and by, to reassess his thinking
on this especial want, this chocolate egg.

– 'This chocolate egg'! Ha! A lucky escape!
Thank God for skinheads! – those kinds of thoughts,
compensations, lonely, in the street.

Of course, the problem with a half-mile walk
is that it takes a half to make it home,
to make a mile. He sighed, and turned a U.

Perhaps it was time to put that treat behind him,
to concentrate on proper evening food,
something good-for-you, something good.

XIX

Well hell – it happened so fast – where do you start?
Let's see what people said, then what they did
when the unpleasantness occurred that recent

Saturday – Wayne said they'd 'sort 'im out';
Bruno concurred in that – instead they sat
speechless, motionless, as he strode through

the crowded Dog and Barrow – the skinhead –
wielding something small and probably
vicious – but they sat and stared at him,

and the girls saw him late, his ex was last
of all to see the start of a long arc,
his armed hand scything through the smoke

to land, a bird, in her red spiky nest
with an endangering squelch: and to recede,
leaving its botch of brown, yellow, white,

egg-resemblers melted to the facts –
Protein, Carbohydrate, mostly Fat –
sticky highlights in a shock of hair.

The skinhead backed away, his hand a mess,
but somehow a successful mess, and anyway,
he wiped it on the codger's head. The boys

were on their feet, but powerless to piece
the chocolate into egg. 'I love yer, Clare,'
the skinhead hoarsely cried. 'Fuck off,' said Clare,

XX

watching him leave the pub, and in fact her life.
But bashing into someone's yet again –
the homecoming and optimistic bloke,

49

TIME in hand, an evening meal to make,
a friend to find, perhaps a girl – but no,
a burping skinhead telling him where to go,

telling him where to put it, telling him 'Oh,
I love 'er, she's my girl!' and vanishing
lurching down an alley, and then quiet.

And then a stranger crossing the quiet street
towards him, a girl, nobody he knew.
He looked behind him, trying to work out who

it was she was approaching. It was him.
'I'm hiding it,' she said, in her disguise.
She gave it to him, looked into his eyes,

brown as hers, but no one said a thing,
and two moments too many passed: she turned
and hurried off. He opened his right hand:

golds and reds in the streetlight – the last
unconsumed and still-desired delight…
The bloke looked up, the girl dodged out of sight,

but followed him until he closed his door,
still very puzzled. Then she hurried home.
The bloke began unwrapping in his room.

XXI

O Egg, your garments are of gold and scarlet!
Egg, you have that brown aroma! Egg,
you look so small but you can fill all holes!

But I don't need to eat you! You have nothing
my body needs, you may do lasting harm!
You cost too much, you're fattening! You're mine!

Outside on Meat Street, where the Market was,
the awnings flapped, the rain quickly began,
the advertising hoardings wrinkled. One,

the largest-ever, the one for Chocolate Eggs,
was such a vast expanse of paper, the rain
overweighted it. An upper corner

peeled from the wall, and the rainwater
sliced behind the sheet, bringing it down
slowly, magisterially, to earth

to swamp the market-stalls, a white tarpaulin.
The first twelve men to notice this rushed on
regardless, but a thirteenth phoned his boss

who carried on as normal, in his bath.
Night fell. Put it another way: England
spun out into darkness, didn't count,

didn't have the sun, had all the rest.
What else? The bloke, (my hero, I admit)
scoffed the thing and didn't die of it.

Farm Close

The small field by my house is the small field
I mean: the old green field of incidents,
small teams, comments, and the planned insult.

It's just the same to look at, like my book
with the Straw-Witch on page 9, the frightener!
It doesn't frighten me, but nothing does.

On the small field now, different goalkeepers
minding their own when the quarrel starts
and different bullies asking, but still doomed

to weeks in jail or profits in South London.
Different targets too, but they deserve it,
and I feel towards them like the ones we had.

Just drab men punching in the rain.
For me to stop them, stop the usual hurt,
would be to disrupt the business of a town,

or change the future of a small, determined planet.
And I'm just the mad beloved Time-Traveller
who, as you probably know, can't do that.

from

OUT OF THE RAIN

(1992)

Errand Boy

To amble on on the brightening, clouding
pavement to happen to pass whom he wants,
    innocently, to pass involves
passing his home with feigned indifference
and moving on, nowhere left to be heading.

She is the brown bare-armed au pair,
her charges holding her hands. Though he really
    means his major smile at them,
it is all in his own and other way fairly
for her, and their voices are English and clear

as they fade, hers neither as it also fades.
And now he's stuck on an imaginary errand, which
    seems to be suddenly unimportant
from the way he slows down and checks his watch
then monitors interesting forming clouds.

The Fires by the River

Just say you went beside the fires by the river,
in neither night nor day, insofar as
violet and lime were the shades of the air that
      steamed or anchored over
the slurping water, and this was the River Thames
      you somehow knew it.

And people had turned to people of those days,
though moreso, now you walked and heard
the actual cursing, the splattered effluents,
      not far from you in the rose-
grey coloured mud that sloped to the pale Thames
      to be its banks.

Just say the place was a mezzanine or less
up from hell, and who wasn't a thug was a child.
And there was a drug called drug, and a drug that went
      by day in a blue guise;
and there was a boat of cocktailers on the Thames
      staring at this point –

at lolling homes, and clapboard warehouses
shot with mice or riddled with the likes
of Monks and Sikes, who mutter by the wharf –
      skin-crawling passages –
all, just say so, that was real as the Thames
      is, by any life:

what would you do with your clean hands and drowned
feet in the place? Remove them to a room?
Remove them to a room. And sit, forget
      the city-licking sound
of water moving slowly through the Thames
      like years in thought.

EC3

Her heart alert and in on things she walks
quickeningly by my side. Her looks
are mirrored dustily on glass that mirrors
crane and ruin high over her. She *is*
      the Eyecatcher. This *is*
      the real City. Some terrors

for me are terrors for her but look how the dust
of drilled churches skips her with a gust
that blinds old me. I blink into all men
dressed as what they are and were all day
      and were all yesterday
      passing neglecting on, un-

der irredeemable heights of rocking steel.
I'd scurry from so high, or seem to kneel
from gap to remaining gap towards remains.
She guides by this, blonde of a village past,
      glancing noticed past.
      My interested remains

hurry on beside what eyes still go
up, down, up, down hopefully and no,
through one bulb-lit and tiny violet cave,
then out between the vital youngster drunk
      and useless ruin drunk,
      where leaden, beaten love

does with what it has. This *is* the mile
ahead. Abandon stabs at it. These pale
scuttling creatures under the high nod
of the pudgy near-to-dead are in it now.
      We thread on by it now,
      exchange the affecting nod

and pass below, away to our ticking homes.
No nothing in the tallest of my dreams
'll grow as tall as, falling up and down
as that, or hook these red uncrediting eyes
      like the Eyecatcher's eyes
      in the dead east of town.

The Eater

Top of the morning, Dogfood Family!
How's the chicken? How's the chicken?
Haven't you grown? Or have you grown,
here in the average kitchen at noontime
        down in the home, at all?

Bang outside, the bank officials
are conga-dancing and in their pinstripe
this is the life! But it isn't your life
out in the swarming city at crushhour
        dodging humans, is it?

Vacant city – where did they find it?
Blossom of litter as the only car
for a man goes by. When the man goes by
his girl will sulkily catch your eye:
        will you catch hers?

Snow-white shop – how do they do that?
Lamb-white medical knowing and gentle
man, advise her, assure and ask her:
do you desire the best for your children
        and theirs? Well do you?

Take that journey, delight in chocolate,
you won't find anyone else in the world,
lady, only the man, the sweet man
opening doors and suggesting later
        something – what thing?

Short time no see, Dogfood Family!
How's the chicken? How's the chicken?
How have you done it? Have you done it
with love, regardless of time and income
        and me? Who am I?

I am the eater and I am the eater.
These are my seconds and these are my seconds.
Do you understand that? Do you get that,
you out there where the good things grow
        and rot? Or not?

The Uninvited

We did not care muchly who, in the murder,
we turned out to be, providing whoever
used to inhabit the white chalk figure
frozenly pawing the blood-stained sofa
was not one of us but a different dier.

Dazzled colonel, distracted lover,
meddling couple of the library whisper,
cook unpoisoned or ponderous super,
sleuth, inheritor, innocent, actual
killer detected or undetected – it

didn't matter, but not that ended
individual manning the hour
he died in, as we would all one *dies*
man one hour, one mo, one jiffy.
Let us be Anybody other than Body!

But then we'd go on with the game all summer:
the three allowed queries on the hot verandah,
the fib in the gazebo, the starlit rumour,
the twitching curtain and the dim unhelpful
gardener's boy: it would all be explicable

soon in the lounge, and we didn't mind waiting.
No, what we minded was the hairless stranger
who wasn't invited and wouldn't answer
and had no secrets or skeletons either,
and got up later than us, then later

than even the bodies, and never turned in,
or blamed or suspected or guessed the outcome
but always was exiting, vanishing, going,
seen on the lawn – then there were more of them
massing, unarmed, parting when followed,

combing the country but not for a weapon
or corpse or clue, then halting and singing
unknown thunderous hymns to a leader
new on us all at our country party he'd
caught in the act of an act of murder.

Recollection of a Meal

She was rich in her own right.
So that either deigning to dance the slow flamenco
on any saint's day or getting her tanned arms dirty
a while at the hovering farm, she – one knew no
reason for pity really.

I got there much too early.
She showed what we could eat at the beginning,
then what we could choose at the end, and I said shyly
how very nice it all looked and this from a young
male like me isn't easy

but she looked anywhere but.
At the tall retainers and Rheinweins, at a diplomat
the black of whom was somehow a different black
from that of the lot you could make out inching back
from dull, bloodying work.

All talk was of the big bear
trapped in the heart of her ancestral forest
that very morning, early. The hussar
had seen it and was laughing, crying 'Honest!'
to them all and then to her.

Flies met on the high ceiling
over the grand dining and didn't move.
The ploy, that luring lemon pool, was ideal.
I began on the fragile squirting starter. 'In love?'
I gripped my fork. 'Well?' Ill.

'Plague?' I picked my spoon up,
glancing the eachway glance at the nodding and roaring
neighbours as long as the eye could glance, then fixed
both eyes on the plate and shells and name, daring
a trembling hand and one sip

of a hot notorious best
below its guiltless foam. That made me a starman,
instantly and confidently modest,
sharing my experience, my mouthful charm, and
settling in as a hinting guest

to the acceleration
of the meal – a dab, the slick hands coloured orange
easing the picked-at plates away, the aimless
flirt with the diagonally-across-from-me angel,
my falling, filling wineglass,

the arriving topped desserts,
bries and dolcelattas, unsealed, bulging.
But my grand exit, to the sea-green marble *Gents*
where ambassadors sighed and punned in the pungent
echoey air, was my chance –

to wait for her own polite
exit to where she'd have to go, via where
I stood, and then to comment, and to light
her cigarillo, and not seem to care
even as she'd hurry by

and on into the yellow
alabaster *Ladies*! Would you credit
she never came? Too rich to be so empty,
surely to God, she was rich in her own right,
but no, she never met me

again and I doggedly made
sure of that: when the minks filled and collected
outside the cloakroom, I was calm and hid,
and when the glassy table clearly reflected
her face, I was under it

amusing the gathered cats.
They did for the fallen food while we all waited
for her to swish out. It's a piece of piss to look back
and label it, like 'fin de siècle' – admit it,
we are gods at retrospect –

but did she deserve what came?
You'll say: 'She never deserved what she had.' Okay,
I'll say the same. Okay. And anyway, I'm
now remembering faces on that Sunday,
straw-sucking, open, dumb,

marooned by the shut gates.
And I wasn't awfully well, and the so-rich food.
And she was only so beautiful. And those cats
they did look peckish, and the diplomats were rude
as graffiti. One forgets.

Although, when one enjoys and
is eating during an era, one scarcely thinks
of the next one, does one? Think what would have happened!
She'd have to have stripped the ladies of the minks,
opened the french windows

for the day workers, freed
those flies, then let the sad grizzly's ankle
out of its clotting ring, then disagreed
in different ways with every banker's angle,
then understood what the dead

were on about. Equally,
I'd have to have jumped her by the door for *Dames*,
hooded her, pulled her, thrown her in the back of my
2CV and motored to kingdom come,
telling her why on the way.

Helene and Heloise

So swim in the embassy pool in a tinkling breeze
The sisters, *mes cousines*, they are blonde-haired
    Helene and Heloise,
One for the fifth time up to the diving board,
The other, in her quiet shut-eye sidestroke
Slowly away from me though I sip and look.

From in the palace of shades, inscrutable, cool,
I watch exactly what I want to watch
    From by this swimming pool,
Helene's shimmer and moss of a costume, each
Soaking pony-tailing of the dark
And light mane of the littler one as they walk;

And the splash that bottles my whole life to today,
The spray fanning to dry on the porous sides,
    What these breathtakers say
In their, which is my, language but their words:
These are the shots the sun could fire and fires,
Is paid and drapes across the stretching years.

Now Heloise will dive, the delicate slimmer,
Calling Helene to turn who turns to see
    One disappearing swimmer
Only and nods, leans languorously away
To prop on the sides before me and cup her wet
Face before me near where I'd pictured it.

I was about to say I barely know them. –
I turn away because and hear of course
    Her push away. I see them
In my rose grotto of thought, and it's not a guess,
How they are, out of the water, out
In the International School they lie about,

What they can buy in the town, or the only quarters
Blondes can be seen alighting in, and only
        As guided shaded daughters
Into an acre of golden shop. 'Lonely?'
Who told me this had told me: 'They have no lives.
They will be children. Then they will be wives.'

Helene shrieks and is sorry – I don't think – my
Ankles cool with the splash of her sister's dive:
        I wave and smile and sigh.
Thus the happiest falling man alive,
And twenty-five, and the wetness and the brown
Hairs of my shin can agree, and I settle down.

'Already the eldest – suddenly – the problems.
The other draws, writes things.' I had heard
        Staccato horrid tantrums
Between earshot and the doorbell, held and read
Heloise's letters in chancery
Script to her dead grandmother, to me,

To nobody. They have a mother and father,
And love the largest pandas in the whole
        World of Toys. The other
Sister rang from Italy and was well,
But wouldn't come this time. 'She'll never come.
She has a home. They do not have a home.'

Stretching out in her shiny gold from the pool,
Heloise swivels, and sits and kicks
        Then reaches back to towel
Her skinny shoulders tanned in a U of lux-
Uriant material. Helene
Goes slowly to the board, and hops again

Into the dazzle and splosh and the quiet. Say,
Two, three miles from here there are heaps of what,
        Living things, decay,
The blind and inoculated dead, and a squad
Of infuriated coldly eyeing sons
Kicking the screaming oath out of anyone's.

Cauchemar. – We will be clear if of course apart,
To London again me, they to their next
    Exotic important spot,
Their chink and pace of Gloucestershire, Surrey, fixed
Into the jungles, ports or the petrol deserts.
I try but don't see another of these visits;

As I see Helene drying, Heloise dry,
The dark unavoidable servant seeming to have
    Some urgency today
And my book blank in my hands. What I can love
I love encircled, trapped and I love free.
That happens to, and happens to be, me,

But this is something else. Outside the fence,
It could – it's the opposite – be a paradise
    Peopled with innocents,
Each endowed with a light inimitable voice,
Fruit abundant, guns like dragons and giants
Disbelieved, sheer tolerance a science –

Still, I'd think of Helene, of Heloise
Moving harmless, shieldless into a dull
    And dangerous hot breeze,
With nothing but hopes to please, delight, fulfil
Some male as desperate and as foul as this is,
Who'd not hurt them for all their limited kisses.

We Billion Cheered

We billion cheered.
    Some threat sank in the news and disappeared.
It did because
    Currencies danced and we forgot what it was.

It rose again.
    It rose and slid towards our shore and when
It got to it,
    It laced it like a telegram. We lit

Regular fires,
    But missed it oozing along irregular wires
Towards the Smoke.
    We missed it elbowing into the harmless joke

Or dreams of our
    Loves asleep in the cots where the dolls are.
We missed it how
    You miss an o'clock passing and miss now.

We missed it where
    You miss my writing of this and I miss you there.
We missed it through
    Our eyes, lenses, screen and angle of view.

We missed it though
    It specified where it was going to go,
And when it does,
    The missing ones are ten to one to be us.

We line the shore,
    Speak of the waving dead of a waving war.
And clap a man
    For an unveiled familiar new plan.

Don't forget.
    Nothing will start that hasn't started yet.
Don't forget
    It, its friend, its foe and its opposite.

The Hang of It

Hugh it was who told me, didn't tell me,
Showed me, wouldn't let my hands on his

Cowboys or Confederates, Hussars,
Saxons, Romans, Japanese:

'This is where they go,' he said, gasping
Eight-year-old whom I remember then

Looking like he probably does now he's
Got a boy himself. I sat there, six.

He stood them where they stand, huge forces,
Squares and oblongs ranged along a gap, a

No-man's table, polished, with a face
Blinking off it, his, with his whole mouth a

Fogging chocolate breath. 'Now,'
He breathed, 'for the big planes, they always start it.'

I didn't disagree but was amazed
When start it was exactly what they did

And finished it in twenty seconds. 'Hugh,'
I hazarded: 'that took an hour to do.

But look at it all now.'
He did, nodding, picking out the blue

Yankees from the silver-painted Danes.
'I'll let you have one go, if you're quite sure

You've got the hang of it.' I took the hour
To set it up and of course he walked in

Saying 'Wrong, wrong, wrong, Glen,'
But picking up his planes.

Sport Story of a Winner

(for Alun and Amanda Maxwell)

He was a great ambassador for the game.
                                    He had a simple name.
His name was known in households other than ours.
                                    But we knew other stars.
We could recall as many finalists
                                    as many panellists.
But when they said this was his Waterloo,
                                    we said it was ours too.

His native village claimed him as its own,
                                    as did his native town,
adopted city and preferred retreat.
                                    So did our own street.
When his brave back was up against the wall,
                                    our televisions all
got us shouting, and that did the trick.
                                    Pretty damn quick.

His colours were his secret, and his warm-up
                                    raindance, and his time up
Flagfell in the Hook District, and his diet
                                    of herbal ice, and his quiet
day-to-day existence, and his training,
                                    and never once explaining
his secret was his secret too, and his book,
                                    and what on earth he took

that meant-to-be-magic night in mid-November.
                                    You must remember.
His game crumbled, he saw something somewhere.
                                    He pointed over there.
The referees soothed him, had to hold things up.
                                    The ribbons on the Cup
were all his colour, but the Romanoff
                                    sadly tugged them off.

68

We saw it coming, didn't we. We knew
                    something he didn't know.
It wasn't the first time a lad was shown
                    basically bone.
Another one will come, and he'll do better.
            I see him now – he'll set a
never-to-be-beaten time that'll last forever!
                    Won't he. Trevor.

Dream but a Door

Dream but a door slams then.
Your waking is in the past. The friend
who left was the last to leave and that
left you, calm as a man.

Wash in a slip of soap belonging
only a week ago to a girl but
yours now and washed to a nothing.
As you and she, friends and not.

Eat to the end as toast,
the loaf she decided on, only last
Saturday last. The crust is what
you said you'd have. So have.

Stop by the calendar, though,
and peel. The colour today
is yellow, and you will never remember
what that means – 'J'.

Drink to the deep the coffee, down
to the well of the dark blue cup.
The oaf with the nose of steam is alive
and well again. Look up.

Desire of the Blossom

This strain bloomed red. It became tended:
Admirable, colourful, a flower
In the good corner. No more green wildfire
Threatening no promising: that
    Pollen-coaxing
Act had ended.

And eyes had me, noses neared and dwindled.
Cameras' mutated insect heads.
Partakers came to tag all sorts of reds
They marked in me: Royal Mail Red,
    Robin and Blood-Red,
Vigil Candle,

Ibis, Ripper, Cardinal and Crab-
Apple. Then they went and I remain
This pleased awhile, in a glow – sane,
Boiling with their help, cooled
    Fitfully by the night
And the dew-web

Nagging me woken, wired, sustained – red.
But say, of a morning, may I, (dreamt I), one
Morning shake like an animal in rain
These ribbons off and look
    A neglected species
The colour Mud?

Cause if, I would remove to a far garden,
Cold, unphotogenic, dry to the sight,
Proffering no petal, no respite
From strict time, then ugly,
    Vegetable, fibrous,
Strain and harden.

Rare Chat with the Red Squirrel

No even now, when your
once astonished, once muttering, once
blurting, lastly listening faces group
and grey in a demi-circle in this home garden,
I can surprise you.

Not with my rare colour,
– you protest at 'rare', you who had, yes you,
pinned me down on your recto 'Extinct in England',
and you who scribbled 'hoax' when you even saw me,
manning the riddled elm,

or after, at my capture,
sniffed round me like a wine-sharp, or a
buyer about to nudge his honey and show her
'you see this is painted on' – but even then
you wouldn't have it:

you merely substituted
'common' then, like it made you less the wrongdoer,
envisaging squads of us and I the ringleader
swiftly nailed. You wouldn't believe a murmur
on my bushy red honour.

Nor when the grey,
fresh from his walnut elevenses,
bared his teeth at the bars till the cops inferred
yes, I was that victim and made me feel so
strangely guilty

as he was handled away,
and I said 'You dig, that wasn't the actual grey
who did my nutkin over – he was another,
and I'd know his red eyes anywhere, 'cause
hell, I'm in them', no,

you caged me again,
and locked and stood and pondered what I did.
It was sodding dark in there with my surname's red
uncaught by light, so nothing. I cocked my head
for one measly eureka

but the way it went was, like,
a burning bath to see if my red would leak,
an X-ray into what was making me talk,
a bastard prod to see what made me not talk,
a mugshot, an APB –

fine, fine way to love me.
But gentlemen, ladies, that is the better-left-
unsaid past you notice I always say.
You would too, but let us enjoy this day.
Everybody looks grey

who waits in the oaks
and ashes for that time when with my eyes
hurt on a text, and nuts beside my nut-tray,
Nature takes her run-up and I'm quick with love
but not quick enough, so,

in the long mean time,
listen only to how the noise you hear
in your wide language differs in no respect
from what you heard when I first happened on nut,
or burst from the grey horde

who got the rest, for I know
you listen to me not for a new wisdom,
nor music nor aloneness in my England,
and nor for what remains of my red coat,
nor that you thought me dead,

though that perturbed you
maybe a little, no? You know it's only
my bound, hic and squeak when I rub my eyes.
Beats me why, cross my heart, but it's a song
you should recognise.

Plaint of the Elder Princes

(for David Maxwell)

We are the first and second sons of kings.
We do the most incredibly stupid things.
   When we meet Elves
    We piss ourselves;
When we see adults walking around with wings,

We crack up laughing and we take the mick.
We wind up in a cloud or we get sick,
   Or turned to stone,
    Or wedding a crone
And running widdershins and damned quick,

Or otherwise engaged, up to our eyes.
We brag, we stir, we mock and we tell lies.
   Upon our Quest
    Eight Kingdoms west
We find no peace: nobody evil dies.

No, seven Witches have a Ball and go to it.
Our sweethearts meet a toad and say hello to it.
   We bet it's our
    Brother De-ar:
It is, we ask a favour, he says no to it.

We are the first and second sons of Queens.
We have our chances and our crucial scenes
   But it comes up Tails
    While Our Kid scales
The castle walls with some wild strain of beans

To make his dream come out. What about ours?
We've wished on every one of the lucky stars:
   Got on with Wizards
    And off with Lizards,
Sung the gobbledegook to Arabian jars,

But no: we serve to do the right thing wrong,
Or do the bad thing first, or stagger along
    Until it's time
    For the Grand Old Rhyme
To drop and make our suffering its song.

The Fool implied that we were 'necessary'
In his last lay. This made us angry, very.
    Perhaps we are,
    But his guitar
Has found a lodging quite unsanitáry.

'Typical Them!' we hear them say at court:
'Brutal, selfish, arrogant, ill-taught!'
    They thought we would
    Turn out no good
And lo! we turned out just as they all thought,

We first and second Princes of the Blood.
Dreaming of a woman in a wood.
    Scaring the birds,
    Lost for words,
Weeds proliferating where we stood;

But hell, we have each other, and the beer.
Our good-for-nothing pals still gather here
    To booze and trample
    And set an example
From which the Golden Boy can bravely veer.

We're up, and it's a fine day in the land.
Apparently some Princess needs a hand.
    It's us she wants?
    Okay. This once.
Show us the map. This time we'll understand.

Rumpelstiltskin

'Your name is Rumpelstiltskin!' cried
The Queen. 'It's not,' he lied. 'I lied
The time you heard me say it was.'
'I never heard you. It's a guess,'

She lied. He lied: 'My name is Zed.'
She told the truth: 'You're turning red,
Zed.' He said: 'That's not my name!'
'You're turning red though, all the same.'

'Liar!' he cried: 'I'm turning blue.'
And this was absolutely true.
And then he tore himself in two,
As liars tend to have to do.

One and Another Go Home

The One flies back to his land and it dubs him King;
    the Other flies back to it too,
and glimpsed in a thicket of glancing heavies is fair
pummelled to yellow and blue and bloody good thing.

But he lives, and the sun comes up on the worked land
    lethally warm and sweet
at each a.m., and up in the loft of the future
the One and the Other meet, avert, demand,

force an agreement, a modus vivendi, a plan.
    The One shall stand for all
the hope and story of the People, the random
flame in the ancient hall and the grants of Man,

and stand for them still, still as the harvests shrink,
    and predatory neighbours
salivate on the banks, while too many children
have too many hungers, townships thrashing sink,

and the thought-out complex effort is too complex,
    too like an effort, too slow,
its answers long and slow, its questions endless,
and the One won't know, flee to or from bare facts,

be webbed as any would be in the net of how
    on earth any earth can suffer
an infinite dark increase at the rim of the meal –
while gnawing a bone the Other, remembered now,

in all four corners of counties, on all fours,
    will wait his turn until
enough are dismayed enough to muster and cry
'Whose fault is it all?' at which he goes 'Not yours.'

La Brea

Los Angeles. So just
guess what I saw: not the dust
or the wide jammed road, not that. And not
the park where enormous playthings eat

the shouting children. No, and the glass white
televised cathedral? – that
was a sight seen for the sin-
gle flashed moment, and gone.

I saw the tar-pits at La Brea,
where a dark endowed museum squats, and where
the thick blots of lake are watched,
and the haired replicas stroked and touched

by kiddies. There's a tour:
the intelligible stone, the Short-Faced Bear,
the Dire Wolf, American Lion and Mastodon,
and Man with not much brain.

Well they did all make a dumb
choice that day! But my day was warm
and fascinating. Try to see these
tar-pits, in La Brea, in Los Angeles.

Nativity

Town of a hundred thousand hands
Locks in for snow. The sky goes somehow
Orange and green, orange *and* green
    As the animals go where animals go:
    Away, behind, due south, below.

Flaring in freshening welcome dusk
Like matches struck the Nativities glow,
Curl in the sight of arriving boy,
    Chorusing parent, mouthing girl,
    Stressed and entire the infant world.

The mirrors are framed with the lights they mirror:
They people and double the rooms with infinite
Manifestations of a bright none other.
    'For one to appear!' cries someone there,
    So close to expecting it, eyes to the air.

Moments when what no longer matters
Is actually Time and incredibly Money
Visit on towns of ten to ten million,
    Swoop like a targeting bird from an eyrie,
    As furiously quickly, as over, as scary.

Who saw it all stamp. Over the writer
Hovers that quiet that started as answer,
Aged to a question, ended as quiet
    But sensed, as the animal everywhere sense
    Sudden, distinct, involving events.

War Hero

Where recollections end,
    step finally from the land
and into the white before like the masked birdman,
a boy is bound to appear:
    growing, hurrying here
over the hot dry grass towards his grandad.

He, who fought on the Somme,
    wanted to see the same
storm damage, down the road on a meadow,
as did this boy of five.
    The sky all blue above.
Was there a storm? morning enquiring. Never.

I caught him up on the road.
    'Look at the oak,' he said,
and sure enough it was peeled to the root by lightning
we'd both seen. Its scar
    was fierce white. Nowhere
could we see the bark tracked clean off with a fork.

He wouldn't touch the sore.
    'Reckon it's hot there.'
Anything else he reckoned or said about it
he carried onto his flight,
    climbing, level in sunlight,
to Lancashire summers beyond the hideous river.

And Leaves Astonishing

For now, among the falling of the ochres,
Reds and yellows, in which haze the many
    Casualties of what on earth
Went on here this month, re-fuse, this joker's
Pockets open out and he digs for money.

His the face suggested to, spat on,
In which the door and final door were shut,
    The mother of which saw and lost
At stations, and the quizzes of the Western
Shows made to a shape you don't forget:

Human of the Revolution, soul
We would wouldn't we be if our dreams
    Loomed amateur cine of tanks
Slowing round our corner and the whole
Hope thing holed and fumbling in own homes –

For now he buys and smokes and his rivered mug
Grins above the inhalation. It all
    Rustles by beyond him now,
The elbowing to run the show, the lag
Of bloody onus, economic stall,

The eloquence and begging in the States
And books of what it was, means, portends.
    Photographed and asked, he moves
His hand to – what, to offer cigarettes
Nobody takes. He takes and lights one, stands

And leaves, astonishing the siding rich
With just being. The love sticks on the tongue.
    He goes his way, who went his way,
Where talk is meant and lit, at the throat's hutch,
On streets of blood, in cafés of the lung.

Didymus the Seated

Without a shadow of doubt,
Debate on Whether or Not has ad infinitum
Filled to the roof an auditorium: risen
Velveted podia, strung an array of mikes
As if for a leisurely doo-wop over the footlights
        Of a hired Victorian stage;

But in this blurting age,
More to the taste of the open holes of the horde
Is a boom, a spot, a cue, a one word roared,
Repeated, roared, chanted, sung to a drum
Or klaxoned over a sloping sea of foam
        Until it's all there is.

From time to time to this
Comes one who outwrinkles most by his or her
Inclination to frown or to crinkle, or
Otherwise to do what is other than gaze with love,
Cry real tears, want what you have to have,
        Or join in the deafening noise

To make the obedient choice.
He or she or once in a blue moon they
Can share in the field of silence after the sigh,
Keeping their thinking hushed in the crypt of selves
While the world's liars accomplish nothing by halves,
        Or they can be the one

Insufferable citizen
Who multiplies life anew by the any question
That turns the globe of the screamingly loving a system
Back to a stage and a measly being whose job
Is trying to be very big and have a club.
        Remember, St Thomas,

The Disciple Didymus,
Was alone not in his being the only one
To disbelieve without proof (the other ten
Had seen: they had no choice but to believe):
But left in the cave he furrowed his brow with love
    And wondered with reason.

In this mendacious season,
Find the compelled attentive child who is staring
Not at the idol but at the standing cheering.
Do not disturb or remove him from his chair.
Tiptoe in jeans up the aisle and say in his ear:
    There is a saint for doubt.

Springs of Simon Peter

In a town in which to have tried three times
he rose and he spent such afternoons
    between his friends,
    at Jim's and Tom's
and out, having so chuckled of each
to the other he'd never be out of touch.

Days were for blame and invite; nights
were many though he could have had more, he reckoned,
    and every second
    was up in lights
but he tottered home and peered at his board
for messages, and the word was LORD.

And then it was blank and always so,
a tabula rasa coloured lavender
    only. The calendar
    had less to show
as he riffled it forwards. Here came Jim
but he'd gone by then, when here came Tom.

The next fresh four a.m. he was treading
deazil around the Lake and the thought
    in his head was what
    he was clearly reading
on stones, dates and pages, an ache
to hear, register, shiver, and speak

to stranger and stranger, mentioned, shunned,
a punchline: he would wait in the dust
    all night for the first
    and freezing sound
of the barracking cock, and a surge of sudden
what? then home to his hissing garden

and huge, turning keys. In a town
in which to have tried three times he would lie
    as the very day
    would break, with his fawn
long arms hiding the falls of his face
from his own words spreading through the whole of space.

Thief on the Cross

How are you doing on yours, my pal
in crime? Are you off where the hurt has hurt so far
      it's what life is, and before
was all the goners like us will ever cop
      of paradiso? Well?

Or are you flapping away in the three
agonies, my apprentice? Is that what
      fixes your look on the flat
world we were caught and tried in, makes you turn
      lollingly from me?

Why ever it is – is it your lips?
dry as the lot will be by the squawking dawn,
      dusty as all by noon? –
you've barely cracked a word in our lingo since
      that tin-tiled cyclops

pegged us to our final form,
condemned by imperial thieves to peg as thieves,
      unmissed. Those wailing wives
are crawling back to the feet of our mate in front:
      that triples the hurt for him

in any case. I'm glad we two
purloined a moment's peace from the long pain
      it turned into. Not again –
you're going to ask him again, aren't you? Aren't you
      satisfied? I tell you,

feckless snivelling rascal whelp:
we're only smack bang where our blessed old dears
      predicted, all those years
gone: but this one isn't one of us lot.
      He's innocent; he can't help.

Out of the Rain

I

The animals went in two by two, but I,
alive elsewhere, had been in the loudest town,

pleading. How do I start to explain to you
what was lost, and how, and even before

the rain that came and came?
Yes, it was fun in town. We've never denied

the length of the silver dresses, the babble and haze
of Friday nights and hell, even Sunday nights,

yes. I'd go into detail but I myself
was bright with it all and tended to misting over

if you see what I mean. My Ex was still around
then, but she wouldn't vouch for this, even if

she'd made into the line herself, and she hadn't.
I hadn't either, and this – this is that story.

II

I do remember the last of the hottest days,
because Brack and I were picked to play for the Jungle.

He scored six and I was awarded the red.
Some of those lofty brothers played for the Town,

while their daddy hammered his embarrassing huge boat
on a day like that! The crowd would watch our match

then turn and laugh at the noise from the harbour. Ha!
Some of their people were out like that, in fact,

couldn't concentrate, and finally
conceded they couldn't win. Gallid walked

tensely to the platform for his shot,
and split the green to a three'er, and in a suit!

We linked our bats and danced to the Winners Bar,
anxious for tall foaming Manzadinkas!

III

I know what you think: that meanwhile He held a trial
of thunderclouds and picked one blacker than black,

and patted its hair and said 'Go On, boy, Go Back
And Bring 'Em Hell!' but no, it was just our luck.

– The Weatherman, anyway, had said
the hot spell wouldn't hold, and of course why should it?

He showed us the LOWs, poised at the edge of the world,
the Weatherman, and he grinned and said 'Good night.'

Then they showed our match! They did a feature
on Gallid, what an old star he was, and they say

they showed Brack and I, falling around on the lawn
some time after eleven. Lucky they did,

really, because we don't remember a thing.
We were out of our little skulls, in the jungle.

IV

Before I finally – hell, and it's been a while –
tell about then, the end of the last dry night,

it's worth remembering what had been going on.
We'd had a shit-hot summer, that's for sure,

and the office guys were free to roll their sleeves
and booze or participate, or both, and did.

There was a song that stayed top of the charts,
wouldn't fucking budge. It was called *I*

Want It Now – interesting thing about that:
they told me the tough little singer was last seen nude

and paddling through the studio, I mean really,
great video, or what? But her band were drowned.

What else – the Town won every bloody game
up to that day. I'm kind of proud of that.

V

The animals. Big question, yes, of course:
How did the son-of-a-prophesying-bitch

find them all? – what's the word – the logistics.
Answer: haven't a clue. We did see lorries

parked on the slip road. There was that night with Coops
and my Ex, she was also Coops's Ex, creeping

up to the lorries and banging them and hearing
nothing. I mean, the hollow bong. So we thought

these had been left behind by some small firm
suddenly gone to hell. So we went home.

In retrospect they must have been full of insects.
And there were the quiet trains.

Haggit's kid kept saying in the morning
'There are trains going by and nobody hears them!'

VI

You're starting to think: morons. But what was suspicious?
We assumed they were fuel trains, the secret ones,

and we weren't about to sully our hands with politics.
Anarchists, we weren't. Arseholes maybe.

But I haven't forgotten the buses.
Green, beige, pink and blue buses,

obsolete, used in the tourist season.
We thought – who wouldn't – the old crock was cashing in

like everybody else. I mean, old Haggit,
bless his last words ('You'll drown') was by that time

selling water, and Coops's surgery
was pay-as-you-enter, pay-as-you-stitch, and I

was preaching at a very slight profit.
All we thought was that he was doing what we were.

VII

I'm trying to read the diaries I had
but it's all smudged, and I have to hum that song

to haul it back. Then there's a certain smell
fumes up that summer like nothing else on earth…

– Burning green leaves, his trees dying the death.
They tried to pass a law, you know, to stop him,

pretending they gave a toss about his woodland
when all they wanted to do was show him he couldn't

do what he wanted any more, because.
Because it was unnerving them, in the heat.

Because they didn't know why he was doing it.
Because, because. Because he was doing it.

They rushed it through. The Council hurried to stop
this outrage, as the last tree was lopped.

VIII

I suppose it's still on the statute-book in some
soaking hell. Where was I? In the jungle,

after the match. There was, I remember now,
a last-night-of-the-show feel to it all,

which I'd know about, as I was no slouch on the stage
either, and our production of *Gomorrah*

was banned at once and played to shrieking houses!
Me, I played the lawyer, my lines were

'Shut up, I don't need to know' and 'No you can't'
and – can't remember, something about a warrant.

Coops was a headless king, my Ex his widow,
and Haggit played himself but not very well.

Good days. But yes, it did feel a bit, you know,
like, what the hell would there be to do tomorrow?

IX

In the Winners Bar there'd been Olde Tyme Oyle,
there'd been Manzadinka by the gallon, Chuice,

Diet Light, pints and pints of Splash,
and all the usual girls between the curtains.

There'd been songs of winning, anthems of the Jungle
Club, there'd been speeches and falling down,

and taunts and chants directed at the Town!
I mean it was quite a night, and I've asked myself:

what the hell did we head to the jungle for?
There was Brack and I, Haggit, the blue winger,

the mascot with his mushrooms, and some girl.
We'd most of us played for the Jungle, but so what?

It didn't mean we came from there, although
the winger did – and that girl, and in fact the mascot.

X

Funny how all in the space of what was maybe
half an hour, everything that was starting

clearly announced it was starting. There was a rumble.
There was a vast boomerang of birds

black against the black-green of the jungle's
drenched sky: there was a second, different rumble.

We had a debate. We were always having debates.
Even out of our tiny heads, we were picking

fair sides to wonder what the hell
the rumbles were, and how far away they were.

The junglies – Brack was calling them that
and right to their little faces – the junglies all

got nervous. The winger, who'd not touched a drop, was sure
the war was starting – 'Or at least two different wars!'

XI

The girl, who'd arrived with somebody nobody knew
and had lost him, or just left him with his drink,

made to speak, but so did Haggit. Then
the girl said 'N-n-no, it's a great

elephant larger than any town!' The mascot
gulped and seconded that, but said it was green.

Then Haggit scoffed, and Brack said, 'That's no elephant,'
as a third rumble came, 'That's my mother!'

And so it was left to me to feel the cold,
and calm them down. 'Sod it, it's just thunder.'

Full marks for irony, of course, but remember,
it had been a good nine months. Then Haggit and Brack

got serious and agreed. Which meant the junglies
were outvoted, as the girl had disappeared.

XII

More obviousnesses then. Sheet lightning.
God's face in it, bored, on His chin.

One of us shouting, 'Knock if off!' to Him.
And suddenly it stopping, at our shins.

'Ahem, let's go home,' ventured Haggit,
wobbling on a log. 'We'll get a chill.'

And we asked the blue winger, who in our game
had played what they call a blinder, to help out

for teammates' sakes, by showing us our way.
Brack was getting jumpy. 'What do you say?

Will you help us out, us three?'
It was very dark. He was speaking to a tree.

'Fucking fairweather friend,' he spat. 'Blue freak!'
And the mascot giggled and we were up shit creek.

XIII

No wonder Brack was losing it: after all,
he was a news-hound, that was what he did.

They'd be screeching for him, threatening his friends
back in the newsroom – 'Where's Brack? IT RAINED!'

He could hardly call in sick, after his great
heroics in the match, and his face in the News:

so he knew he was out of a job.
No of course he didn't know we all were.

Haggit, meanwhile, he had a wife and kid,
who'd certainly be waiting to be angry.

But he was a calm kind of a man, and he said
'Let's work it out from the light.' I said 'What light?'

I do admit I was hardly a help. I kept thinking
of the losers happy in the Winners Bar, drinking.

XIV

We waded where we thought we'd waded from.
We couldn't lose the mascot, who kept saying

'Whistlework, whistlework,' and our only
guide was the one cloud pierced

by the moon, and only at times.
Otherwise it was dark and the only sounds

were the mascot and, ultimately, Brack
drowning it. Then we were worried men

and cold, thinking of lawns and admitting it.
We waded on, it got drier, higher up,

a good sign, for our port was on a hill.
That's why they called us mad, but we didn't choose

to have the sea up there, where the ancient bloke
had made his boat, and we called him mad too.

XV

They called us – not only mad – wait for it,
the Golden Generation. It was our cars,

and our carefree times, our drinks on the roofs of homes,
our tilted velvet hats in the winter, our games

and how we used our leisure, made it work for us,
our softness on ourselves, our relaxed

attitude to money. Most of all,
because we called ourselves Golden. And hell,

good times. But as I say – that last night air:
what would there be to do tomorrow? More.

More of the gazing over the black-tiled floor
for that single someone, more of the same jazz

in all four corners of the cars, and more
seasons of the League, and those hot days.

XVI

We were near the shore. We knew that by the smell
of salt and gull, and sometimes the sound

of breakers but Haggit shrugged and said 'Thunder.'
I didn't think so. Brack

seemed to snag his ankle on each tree
like he was trying to, and the moon came right

out, and we caught each other's eyes. 'Right,'
said Brack: 'this is a nightmare. Pinch my cheek.'

I closed my eyes, while Haggit lost his temper,
and so it was I who heard them – girls' voices.

Drunk as us, drunker than us, moving
towards us not away from us, and many:

Brack said 'This is a dream. Leave me alone.'
Haggit and I just stood. We were shaking.

XVII

A second's realisation of torchlight.
A second second's seeing we were found…

'Hoo, trolls! Look who's been in the rain!
Ahoo, aha! A treasury of wet men!'

'Is it really them?' 'Is it really who?' 'No!
It isn't them, it's men!' 'Where was the party,

and what were you?' There were six or seven of them,
they had cloaks, they were on their way from something, I

actually thought I knew a couple. Anyway,
they were townspeople all right, and I breathed again.

Brack was talking about our match, our win,
and our looking for fun, but Haggit was squatting down

a misery in the water. One girl said
'Did you hear the wars? Did you hear the elephants?'

XVIII

The wind blew. Another girl said this:
'We're swimming out to the Island for tonight!

There's your fun, heroes! Nobody's there
at this time, and we've got some hammocks there

and Manzadinka, yay! out on the Island,
and then in the morning we swim home to sleep.'

I'm not telling you this because they all
died out there – of course they did, they woke

and there wasn't land – I'm telling you why
it sounded such fun, and why Brack said 'Come on!'

and went with them. It's not like he was mad
or irresponsible, I mean, he was,

but he'd lost his job by then, and he had no kids
or wives to speak of. I had to stay with Haggit.

XIX

Then there's a blank time –
Haggit had stopped talking, or when he did

he was talking to Brack, and I said 'He isn't there'
but it's very vague, though I do remember the girls

in their blowing firelight, trying to lure us
into the woods to change our minds, then suddenly

running away in silence. Then the wind
colossal in the trees, and drops again.

All those trees, all those millions of trees.
Could've come in handy. Wish I'd been

elected, in on it, if you know what I mean –
rather than what I was, the last to make it

out of the sea, the miracle in wet clothes.
Swearing oaths.

XX

The animals went in two by two, I saw them –
later, later, after the girls and the lightning

illuminating the black ocean and figures
swimming out to their shrinking island, after

the still mascot, and after the rain resuming,
and the last dry inch of my body, and Haggit's

wild decision to climb to the top of a pine:
'What are you doing? Come down, come down, come down!' 'I'm

staying here till it's over, son. I can see
hundreds of clouds coming. I don't see the town.

Stay on the earth if you have to, but you'll drown!'
'I won't!' 'You will!' 'I won't!' Well I won't rub it in,

but when the wall of water broke the spit
it would have swamped those pines in about a minute –

XXI

but after I started to run, later, I saw them:
I must have been some way inland,

where the country rose again and rather than wading
I splashed through groves and glades – but it was

amazing – a dry risen corridor of light
guarded (I crouched and shook) through which in, yes,

yawn, yawn, in pairs, the animals went,
some still sleeping, some complaining,

one or two reading, others crying,
others terrified by the mauve heavens

or pointing out God to friends who knew it was Him,
I mean who else would show Himself at a time

like this? But it was just a cloud
and it split in half.

XXII

I backed away, and the light drummed on my back
as I ran and ran and just as I decided

to say a prayer before I died, I tripped
and collided with a stone – or with a square.

I had a square in my mind when I blacked out,
and a square in front of me when I was choked

awake by the water rising. It was a garden
path stone, the first of thirty stones

zigzagging up to a door where a Unicorn
asked me the last animals I saw.

'I saw two Zebras. Following two Yaks.'
'What's your name?' the Unicorn wondered.

I gave it. 'Ah, then you missed your place in the queue.
Like us. But we were always going to.'

XXIII

And these in my dazed state were only words,
though you see they stuck. I blinked, and felt

my whole frame lifted on to a warmth
of animal, white, white animal,

– did I say Unicorn? Yes,
a Unicorn, and it was bearing me

out of the rain, into a room of lamps
and beating lives all blurring into a focus.

They were all animals I hadn't seen,
and never did again, though I saw them now.

They all resembled what I knew, but either
thinner, gentler, slower, or a new colour

and I sat in a ring with them whatever they were,
and the Unicorn sat opposite, and said these words...

XXIV

'One day they came and took the Cat, who'd lied.
They left behind the Other, who'd said nothing.

They came again, and took the eating Dog,
while the Other stopped and offered his food, and stared.

They came again, and fooled the Elephant
who wanted to be fooled; the Other didn't.

They took the Fox next, who seemed reluctant,
and told the Other "You stay here on watch."

They took the Jackdaw who was screaming "I!"
which left the Other, quiet, making a nest.

No problem for the righteous Lion: he went,
but the Other was troubled, needed time to think.

When they next came, the Monkey had packed a case,
but the Other, puzzled, had nothing to put in a case.

XXV

Then the Natterjack, told he'd meet a Princess,
leapt in the air, but the Other fell about.

The Owl put down his book, said "I deserve",
and told the Other "I find you don't deserve."

The Pig – you should have seen him – he almost flew!
But the Other couldn't, so wouldn't, but still hopes to.

The Shark was next – and you know this trip was free?
– he paid a million; the Other said "Not me."

The Sheep were hard to separate, but one
went with the ones who went, and the Other stayed

with the ones who stayed. The Snake was next, accusing
the Other so silently he never knew

why he was left behind with the likes of me
and the Other Unicorn, who stayed with me.'

XXVI

And who then came in with towels, which reminded me:
'Why one at a time? I saw double that.'

Which made her laugh. 'We saw you on the news,
we know about your escapades! – but listen:

are you just a drunken Man – or part of the business?
Who were the ones who went?' 'Nobody went

anywhere!' I cried, 'It was just raining!
There'll be a hell of a lot of mud in the morning!

– but nobody died, did they? What are you saying?'
'Oh,' said a huge bird sadly,

'has anyone been doing something odd
recently, in your town? Like, building something?'

'Only the man with the trees, this local twit,
building a sort of – big...oh shit.'

XXVII

I suppose I overreacted. The lines were down
anyway, and the lights were packing in.

They put me to bed a while, which I shared with something
not unlike a Woman, but comprehensible

and with one face. I couldn't sleep. The rain
never let up, and I went downstairs again.

Some of the furrier guests were thinking of
turning in by then, but things like bats,

otters, hedgehogs – brighter colours, though –
began to reminisce, just wouldn't go,

and the mousy thing in the coat just stared and stared
out of the window.

I ended the night at chess with the bored Yeti.
'Did your companion go?' I asked. 'Dunno.'

XXVIII

I must have got my second wind then,
as the next thing I remember is a full

harmonious hum of snoring, in the dark,
ranging from the unhearable to the zurr

of a bearish group in the library, and always
the rain and as I left,

as I stood on the WELCOME mat and said my quiet
'So long' to the left behind, left them,

and ventured out to the light and the first stone,
I saw an extraordinary thing, – I mean,

even by these standards – how the whole
garden and cottage, seething with the asleep,

was a deep deep hole in the sea, and all around
the walls of water poured against the ground!

XXIX

Nobody was disturbed but I – I saw
water, white with fury at this Law,

fall and fountain again, against its will,
leaving us dry and pocketed, a well

of oxygen in what was the end of a world.
The greenness here, the life of it, was so strong

I thought 'Nobody's wrong, nothing's wrong'
and it felt like my first thought, and I felt how the grass

stayed bone dry to the last.
I thought of waking the Unicorns, and just as I

thought to myself 'There are no such things
as unicorns' the water spurted out

and gripped my feet and whirled me up this spout
and onto the flat sea and that was that.

XXX

Day, I guess. The sky was a sagging grey.
Everywhere dead land and debris,

and after swimming in turn to three of the four
horizons of the dome,

I twisted to look at the last, and it had to be home.
Home, though it shouldn't have been, was a high

ridge with its back to the sea,
and the rain would have to have filled the valley before

the town would flood, although by then
it would have done, and had.

So what were left were the roofs, and the high arena
where we did our plays, and also the Heroes Tower

which from these miles seemed swollen at its steeple
like a hornets' nest on a stick. Clinging people.

XXXI

I swam, and thought of the dead. I thought 'They're dead.'
(I was known as a thinker at school, I'll have you know.)

I thought of the things I'd seen, and thought 'I didn't
see those things.' (I was known as a liar, too.)

I swam over trees and everything I had once
run through, and it all seemed much simpler

and, feeling my confidence build, I stood on the water,
which didn't take my weight. I sank, I swam.

It began to rain again, and had always rained.
I imagined the Winners Bar an aquarium.

Which made me think of the match, which led to the thought
of the noise of the hammering father in his harbour,

which led me to scan the horizon
for his boat and zoo, but no, they were gone like him –

XXXII

– to the Dry, the Saved, the Impossibly Full: a book.
Good end for all that wood, I thought, blankly.

Then I caught some floating door
and lay on it, closed my eyes and trusted it:

we would float upsea to the town.
And we floated upsea to the town.

What was left of it, well yes, we've all seen pictures,
but it's really only another view, only

the dead are about and prices have fallen down,
there's no sport played for a while, and the Police

are pally or warn and fire. Charities come,
and interviewers and the place becomes

famous. But – hell, famous for whom?
Well, okay. Nobody this time.

XXXIII

Washed in, I was reckoned dead. When I woke again
I was on dry land on a roof with the whole Council.

In fact I disturbed a debate on the recent crisis,
and the Mayor, about to cast his casting vote,

nulled and voided the meeting. All my fault.
They adjourned to look at the view, and as I crawled

and stumbled back to an upright position, an old
stalwart took me aside and told me 'Oh,

what a great debate it was!
Some insist we're afloat on a floating detached

roof, others that this is the one building
left, i.e. we've been chosen above all

not to, er, and so on.' 'How did you vote?'
'Oh come on, secret ballot, sir, and all that.'

XXXIV

And then I saw all eyes were on me, the one
neither dead, nor drowning, nor on the Council.

So I said 'Here you are – where are the real people?'
A hushed hiatus then, but the Mayor said 'There,

there', and I told him to stuff his sympathy,
but he pointed at where the Tower had been and where

it now was, a rolling log that couldn't
help any of the hundreds trying to grip it

and splashing to matey death, in each other's way.
The Mayor sat down with me,

and they say I suddenly lost it and screamed at him
to go to the house in the wood and help them in,

and find the lot in the boat and scuttle them!
The Mayor looked at his watch: 'Gentlemen,

XXXV

Time is immaterial. We have
a roof, we have about two dozen men,

we have the bust of the founder, which is round...
I reckon that just about makes a troppling ground!'

And so they played, and I looked out to the sea,
and the sea and the dead, the drowning, the dead and the sea,

and then I joined in a while and managed a five-o
before losing out to the Mace-Man's cunning yellow.

'Ha! Not looking, were you?' the Mace-Man roared,
as the rain from heaven pissed on our troppling board.

'It's slackening off', a fielder said. He seemed
curiously blue for a town official,

but hell he was right about that, and the Weatherman stared
up at the sky, and said 'I want to bat.'

XXXVI

By the time we reached half-time the air was only
dirty, a muzzy brown, like a sand but nothing.

The rain was hardly rain, more like a reminder.
The level remained level. The sea was headless.

We were winning 16-9 with a red in the bucket.
I was always, always going to say 'Oh, fuck it'

as I walked and dived and swam and looked back only
to see a half-mile away

the prizes passing from Mayor to Man, and the caps
thrown in the air and to hear,

small on the wind like the smell of men, 'hooray!'
and then a silence, then

'hooray', tinier than can be, and then
'hooray', and silence. Nothing. This is me.

XXXVII

I was born where I knew no man, nor that
the rain would fall, nor end, nor that a boat

would sail away and none that I knew would follow.
All that I knew are gone, and all

that I know I love and is here and knows it will not
know me tomorrow.

I was born, I know, in a town which never
should have been built where it was, but was,

and I live in this same one next to the sea
where nothing changes but is.

But is that one cloud ever going
to move again, as I bat and believe

it will, or is that the sentence passed?
Time has gone, townspeople, townspeople, time is lost.

XXXVIII

I've been working on this page,
for an age, in the sun.

I'll move towards the open window,
place my hands in the sun.

I'll stroll out to the match where we are
winning it in the sun.

We are two points clear in every league there is.
Bar none.

I'll stroll back from the match where we are
coasting home in the sun.

I'll see my Ex through the open window or
someone, tanned in the sun.

We'll love and laugh and win at all we do.
Or have done.

104

XXXIX

'Yes, well I'm an authority on history',
I tell the eight Reserves when I meet them

in the Winners Bar, taking the daily pictures
of one of only how many survivors?

they ask me, but I shake my head: 'No questions!'
They think I'm joking and they shake my hand.

I give a boy an autograph. I gave him it
yesterday. I'll give him it tomorrow.

I wonder what he thinks of me. The Weatherman
goes past. He's out of a job. I say I'm sorry.

Two of the Council, Gingham and Sub-Gingham,
always mention unicorns when they pass me.

They think that's funny. Gennit, the matchwinner,
shuts them up with a look. And goes past me.

XL

Guess what I saw. 'Your Ex? and she was standing
out on the pitch and waving, wearing a silk

she cut with your own money? and she so wanted
you to go up, so you did,

and she spoke in a new way and her silk came down
and all that was there was yours and you married in town!

Am I right? Oh I'm sorry.
What did you see?' Forget it. Don't worry.

The game is starting now, anyway.
Shall we go and see that game? If we win

we'll be two points clear. So I hope we win. If we win
let's go to the Winners Bar, I've a seat there. 'Yeah?

What's your poison?' Manzadinka.
Manzadinka! 'What?' Manzadinka!

XLI

I can see you through this glass,
all of you. Go on, guess, guess,

guess what I saw. No, a weather forecast.
I'm telling you the truth. It was illegal

but they let it happen. 'Oh.' Is that what you say?
Oh? Yes, I overheard it happen.

'And.' Is that what you say?
And? Is that all? Well. And nothing.

Still the same. Yes, you're dead right I'm mad.
I could see you through the glass, you had a horn

and so did he, you were making fun of me.
But tell them, Mr Councillor, who scored

the Double-Green that day, when the Town were out
for two pinks and a fifty – tell them that!

XLII

I wake in a hot morning, and I make
a breakfast for a man who needs a breakfast!

Nothing has changed. I warm the last night coffee
and reread the local paper, where it says

we won and we are two points clear. The sun
is high above my home. Nothing has moved.

We're favourites for the match today. But don't think
for a moment we won't try.

I hope my Ex will phone. I mow the lawn.
I lecture. I once saw a unicorn.

No, two. I turn my personal radio on.
I Want It Now has gone to Number One.

I finish this and put it on the shelf.
I take it down and send it to myself.

from

REST FOR THE WICKED

(1995)

Peter Brook

Let every page
Begin as clean
And end as clear
As stories are
If actors pass
Through pain and grace
To make a stage
Of any place.

Let every word
Be prized enough
Shyly to talk
Or weep with work
Or fail afresh
Towards a truth
That may be heard
Beyond its breath.

Let every gap
And every strip
Of space fulfil
Its hapless will
That all about
Each uttered mark
The matter drop
Into the dark.

Let every line
In ignorance
Of whence it came
Or what's to come
Hold out its hands
Into the breeze
As I do mine
And cling to these.

The Ginger-Haired in Heaven

Sometimes only the ginger-haired in Heaven
can help me with my life. The flock of blondes
is sailing by so painlessly forgiven,
still blinking with love no one understands,

while the brunettes float thinking by the rushes
long after what they chose, long reconciled,
and here, the fair and sandy, all their wishes
half-granted them, half-wish them on a child.

Only the ginger-haired remember this, though:
this sulk and temper in the school of Time,
this speckled hope and shyness at a window
as sunlight beats and blames and beckons. I'm

not coming out. They won't come out of Heaven,
or not until with auburn in the blood
two mortal tempers melt together. Even
then we might stay here if you said we could.

Birth Day

Through light so nursery-bright on a playing field,
Soup-tin red, sea blue when the sea was really,
Greens of the good for you or a game played fair,
She walked with a smile between the deliberate rings
Of the cross good children shyly ignoring her.

Her young black hair was tied back in a headscarf;
She looked ahead at the houses, though her eyes
Were dark and distant with remembered hymns
Begun inside. She was believed by it all,
Now weekdays whirled and the news of a boy or a girl
Joked in her brilliant blood.
                                        And the glamorous cars
In glossy maroons and greens and stripes went by,
And smokers born in a blanket in a grey war

Bought rainbow-shimmering records and sportsman cards,
Bright paperbacks with jazzily slanting words,
Chewed and swore with a grin then stared all around
At the light all cherry colour.
                                        The whole world over
Nations hastily, scrappily, sulkily born
Pretended they'd been sitting there, honest, forever,
And every oblivious woman and innocent man
Glanced up from the work in hand on the world's one town –
Verges, roses, pinning up, setting out, hosing down,
Whatever. Time began.

The Wish

Alone in spoiling it, I said I wish
That I can wish for everything. They said
That's cheating. You've one wish. I said that *is*
One wish. We sat against the paper shed.

They, who had wished for peace on earth, for painted
Chocolate cities, flights to anywhere,
And one strange one to play with *her* (they pointed
To where she did her handstands on her hair,

Her pout flipped to a smile, as if the sky
Would grant what it amused itself to grant)
They pondered, troubled, hot with how and why,
Considering my case. When the bell went

Against my wish and that most amazing field
Began to be abandoned, as that girl
Was falling to her feet, and chocolate filled
The hands and crumbled happily, I was still

Wondering, as I was all afternoon,
If they would grant my wish. When at last they would,
I found myself at my own gate, alone,
Unwishing, backwards, everything I could.

Garden City Quatrains

First day of school. A boy looks through a pane.
This is the end of freedom, not a visit.
The King's Cross-York-Newcastle-Scotland train
Slams through Welwyn Garden and I miss it.

*

1880. Howard, an asthmatic geezer
Home from Nebraska batters down a map.
Says Bernard Shaw, 'What's happening, Ebenezer?'
'Quiet,' says Howard, 'I think I've found a gap.'

*

By all means vanish, shrug and with a sniff
Explain your town is dead, that anywhere
You're not a native must be filled with life.
Remember where you're gone is the thin air.

*

Woods were north. The south was all my schools.
East was alien housing, west I knew.
Start of a poet. All the rest is false
Or true extrapolations of the view.

*

An idiot asks to know the route I run.
I say I start at home, head north until
Ayot Green, then turn back for the town
And home. He scoffs: 'So more or less downhill.'

*

ST ALBANS KILLED WELWYN is what is written
Under the A1(M). And WANKY SHIT.
In the United Kingdom of Great Britain
And Northern Ireland that just about covers it.

*

Our nearest Lord has turned the nearest park
Over to golf. Between his pits of sand,
Six proud walkers hold their thread of path
And stamp it so they know where they can stand.

*

Through marvellous locked gates, one has a view
Of his grand Hall, along a splendid drive.
I saw in early April '92
A poster. Guess. No. Conservative.

*

A Martian Votes in Welwyn-Hatfield

Inhabitants converge upon a shed
One by one all day, to make a cross.
Outside their homes some show their feelings. Red
For really cross, yellow for fairly cross.

*

The Coronation Fountain in the centre
Of town has been switched off. The Council said
It cost too much to run, what with the winter.
[That's enough royal allegory. Ed.]

*

The Observation of Mr Lohn

Before the night begins, my friend and I
Stop outside the autobank. I run
To take out forty quid. We drive away.
'Out stealing from yourself again, eh Glyn?'

*

They lost their nerve in 1970.
'It's neither Welwyn, a garden, nor a city.'
They thought up 'Howardstown' and 'Waverley'
Since nothing had these names and they were pretty.

*

114

Western Garden Citizen, I stand
At midnight in the east and say 'I'm lost.'
But I'm starting to get to know the back of my hand,
At the cost of moving on, which is no cost.

*

Small hours. The tots are in their cots. The old
Are in their homes. The thin Nabisco towers
Snore the malt. Two strangers have and hold,
And, as in real places, something flowers.

*

Who's in the kitchen? London, the life and soul
You weary of, flirtatious, loud, and hot.
A young well-meaning man is in the hall.
He's got his gift and bottle. What have you got?

As You Walk Out One Morning

Brrring. It is the day of your Proposal.
Get up. You're on your own. You are a suitor.
Leave your attic, basement, croft or castle
In AD, BC, either. Doesn't matter.

A to B is indeed the way you are going,
Towards Before, appropriately enough,
As they do say how it wallops your sense of timing,
Twangs that nought-degree meridian. Love.

You note at once that no one is beside you.
Your neighbour said he'd wave, but so far hasn't.
'Our blessings! May our God be there to guide you!'
Your family never said, and their God isn't.

Your street curled up like it shouldn't have been in the sun.
The houses waddled away, and your underclothes
Are hitching home together. You've got on
A suit you never liked and suppose she loathes.

The bus conductor is me. My bus remains
Beside a depot and both are yet to be thought of.
The road likewise is a field and awaits the Romans.
You wear on your wrist a sundial and it's sort of

Stopped. The craft you became superbly skilled in
Over the years is of no use to any.
Your parents have decided against children.
Plantagenets are peering from your money.

The Earth is of course quite flat, and the heavenly bodies
Twinkle explicably. One is as big as a Swatch.
Today they are all gone away, gone away where God is,
Where the dead play whist and the unborn ask can they watch.

Everyman is still on a final shortlist
In that young kingdom, Fellowship and Good Deeds,
Friendship, Knowledge and all of the Devil's hitlist
Are still his friend, and he himself still God's.

116

But you, it is the day of your Proposal.
You feel the Dead Sea lap the palm of your hand.
Your heart is as light, your soul as white as Persil,
The world and weather more like this ordinary brand.

Flatness on which you travel, height that picks you
Out as a Possible, width that introduces
Infinite manners of *no*, and a breath that sucks you
Up to a point: you have all these, and voices.

Voices! Low in the raincloud flutter the wings
Of *what* and *where* and *why*, the loquacious dove
She-said-to-me, that craps these green new findings
You pause to analyse on your own sleeve.

These you have. But, when you search for the face
You swear you pictured, all the others who ever
Put in a brief appearance in that space
Rustle like actresses to the scene, and pucker.

So all that's left of the love that yesterday
Filled the world is a porch with a bell and a wait,
The number-whatever of here – though who's to say
What squiggles mean? – and the yellow or green or white

Or black or some other word of the closed door.
This, when it opens, frames you into a suitor
Earnestly of your century, the Before
Prattling on at the steps of your mouth, and the Future

Playing it clever and cool in your brown eyes.
The Only Girl In The World arrives to assess
Whether the Future infers what the Past implies.
With all respect, don't hold your breath for a yes.

Love Made Yeah

First and zillionth my eyes meet eyes
    unturnable from, unstarable in.
Whoever was marched from the Square of my reason
and to what court, I don't give a hyphen
    va t'en to the King!

Our drapeaux are waving and what's in the offing
    but tears, tribunals and unwelcome aid?
Nothing but glorious, jealous, incredulous,
bibulous, fabulous, devil'll envy us
    love made, love made!

'Yeah,' but you say, with the Press of the planet,
    'Look how it turns out: the heroes felled
in the upshot, the oiliest climb of the customary
bourgeois fuckers as easy as muttering
    argent, ackers, geld...'

Uh-huh, sans doute. But here at the heart
    of the movement I trust my hand in another!
So CNN tells me I'm odds-on to cop it?
That ain't news, guys, I did arrive here
    via a mother.

No, when the Square is dead again, but
    for some oligarchy or puppet or shah,
and I'm banged up and on trial in slippers
for following, wishing on, crediting, catching
    her my star –

don't do the pity. All right, do the pity,
    but that won't happen, believe it from me!
Her eyes are as hot as one needs to ignite
the cave in the human guy. I am hers,
    friends, I am history!

Either

A northern hill aghast with weather
Scolds and lets me hurry over.
Someone phoned to tell my father
Someone died this morning of a
Stroke. The news has tapped me with a
Stick. I vaguely knew his brother.
No one knows where I am either.

Now I'm lost. I don't know whether
This road runs along the river
Far enough. I miss my lover,
Town and all the south. I'd rather
Die than be away forever,
What's the difference. Here's another
Field I don't remember either.

The Boys and Girls of There

(epithalamium, for Stephen and Sarah Mead)

The grasses were as ever the first to know,
    but gossiping they just leant and listened and nodded,
        absorbed it into their posture, and forgot it.

The cedars remembered hearing it once before
    but they hadn't believed it then and did not now,
        when the robin said 'Do you think so?' 'We know so.'

So the robin as brown as earth had nothing to tell
    the few of that desert town, though his chest was taut
        with wanting to, and the oldest woman he met

observed this, stopped, and guessed her improbable guess.
    Silence grew some twenty-four bare arms
        sweeping the road of the town with whispering brooms

till a paler path was cut through a sea of dust.
    Last from the cool dry huts were the vigorous men,
        still proud but with all hope and pity gone,

wiping their palms in anger and terror at this
    sweeping work, then the whole town stared up the lane
        at something striding out of the hammered sun

the shape of a single person bound in a wheel
    that rolled away, and he stayed three days in the place.
        All they remembered afterwards was his voice,

no help to the Romans, less to the man they sent
    from Herod equipped with a looking-glass from China,
        who herded them up and said 'Look I have forever

so take your time.' But what was there to remember?
    Though they might hang for forgetting the words he spoke,
        his name at the very least, the point of his work,

their minds were blank, they were bright but blank, they were bright,
  and all they would say was 'Yes, he was here, he came,'
    and what was his name? 'Ask that bird for his name!'

but the robin as brown as earth flew bursting away
  with something to tell elsewhere, while the cedars sighed
    'Yes, we were wrong, but we abide, we abide,'

and the elders dozed, but a boy and a girl of there
  sprang to each other and stared, for their being apart
    was a wound they would have to mend, and they made a start.

The Boys at Twilight

Alive to the lilac, dead to the blue,
Bees in the act till the lilac's through,
There's a boy with you and a boy with you.

And the boy with you as the sun goes red
And the lamps go rose and the old to bed
Has remembered words you forgot you said.

If the time comes up when the mind is ruled
Then the nastiest face you have ever pulled
Can't winch you clear of his lost new world,

Can't free him or loose him or let him forget
He's the luckiest boy you have ever met
If the time comes up when the heart is set.

You can pass him lies like so much slack.
You can mouth to his bearers behind his back.
You can fake with a passion and love with a knack

It's hopeless. But hopelessness full of hope
Is the serious man on the end of the rope,
Is the ring and the race and the telescope,

Is the gibbering soul at the outhouse door,
Is the flapping aloft and the crawling ashore,
Is the meaning and matching and marching to war

All hopefulness. In the looks of the shy
Look clear through the fog and be certain why
When the galaxy lunges across that sky

The boys flare up with a hapless glow,
And follow it out to a woods they know
Green-smelling and smothered as years ago.

They sleep in the cold unswayable sight
Of all they envisage, the giant delight
That itself feels nothing but a scratching, slight

But not giving up. Oh, wipe them away.
There's a boy tomorrow and a boy today,
Words they are going to remember to say,

Hopes they are going to remember from when
They have no idea but they feel them again,
Who are going to be boys, who have had to be men.

Song of Our Man

By light of what when filtered down
The piling jungle must have been –
    Once – the moon,
Between what stings and what is silent,
Off the undisputed island
    Swarms the dark platoon.

That was some-worse-where we never
Even thought of, chewing over
    The worst things.
These were who, when cracked reporters
Bared the facts at yellow waters
    Glittered in the wings.

Beyond obituary, they
Inhabited what wasn't Day
    Or Book, or Sun.
Or sound. Or the right words for words,
Or anything our old accords
    Were predicated on.

That was them. We knew their track,
That ultimately they would back
    To a red moat:
For there was only this much left,
The valleys stitched, the woods bereft,
    Our man in the last boat.

But what we didn't know, they were.
What we don't believe, they are.
    There they are.
Out floating out and still alive.
We will breathe and cock and drive
    But not, now, far.

Growing Men

Unravelling red carpets for ourselves,
We're nudged and turn and recognise each other
Stooped and grinning. Slowly we straighten up,
Praise to the sky what sky we see in any,
Then stand on these red carpets for ourselves
All stinking good and spreading out like lives.

The lamps were low enough, the riling heat
Was blood itself it fuelled us so fully.
Whoever did this had to and knew how to.
Whoever did this ought to wipe the ceiling,
Because we're taller even than our heat:
We top it now, our temples lit with sweat,

Our heads of jungle hair congealing, set,
Our thoughts old, crackling thoughts. Pick one, pick all.
Discarding all but one you're stuck with all,
You darling gardeners spotlit on a stroll,
You giant bending angels. You are set
To want us. In that moment you forget

Your eyes are not the eye we inch towards.
Your smell is nothing but a mask of rain.
Your mouth is not our dream of the great well,
And we grow stupidly and proudly from you,
Grow coldly, undramatically towards
The best we get: to nod amid the clouds.

For now we sleep or seethe. We are always young,
And always saddening in our eagerness.
Whoever did this ought to break the glass
We'll grow so high, so high we'll see he has –
He broke a star of air when he was young,
Quite carefully, as if he'd wait that long.

Younger Than That Now

(for the Folk at the Barn)

Open the door one crack and you are backstage.
The closest of the bright unanswering faces
You love and know, but away down the crowded passage
They get much gloomier, longer to recognise.
     Your shyly whispered guesses

Widen and die like cigarette fumes in a hall
Of cleanly livers. You did not know you were holding
Your breath when it broke clear, and there is no wall
To touch, there are only inhabited crackling clothes
     And soon the dizzying feeling

That you must walk through here through the way of them all:
The girls of the frozen chorus, the mouthing page,
The hero bare, the jacketed devil, the cool
Chanel of the goddess, the flirt of the woods, pass on
     Away from the terrible stage

That grinds its young in the light or blows them dark
Like birthday candles, move down corridors
Where the murdered glance from a brilliant mirror and back,
By vast and icy rooms with bills of plays
     That call you to old wars,

Past centuries of dresses coldly hung
In line, rich girls speechless at the affront,
And cards of luck and photographs of song
Pinned to a blistered board, pass by the wires
     That lead from what you want

Away to the grids and terminals of power,
Pass by yourself in brown and broken glass,
By planks and crates at the foot of a storage tower,
By what seems rubbish to you but will be of use,
     And then the rubbish. Pass

Right to the end of the theatre, some last
Green paint-spattered chair by a bolted door.
Far from the lives of the young indignant cast
Or wrenching earshot of beloved lines,
    Sit yourself down there.

Feel like a boy the burden tremble and slip.
Empty your pockets of work and empty your ears
And nose and eyes of fashion. Summon up
Whatever remains. If nothing remains amen,
    But blink no appealing tears,

For here you sit in the foreground of the world.
And what you sing in the dark is the plain song
Of men alone: unobservant, innocent, old,
And blue with wonder, and beating a way back home,
    And over before long.

The Stakes

Forget that in the three-fifteen
My love was quartered pink and green,
Had cherry sleeves and epaulettes

And blinkers and a poet's name.
Forget it couldn't fail but came
Nowhere. In the five to four

Forget my love was gold and grey
And thundered recklessly away
But tired and didn't place. Forget

The diamonds and diabolos
And checks and chevrons of all those
Who caught my eye, engaged my hand

And lost my stake. It's ten past five.
My love is emerald-starred, and me I've
Set my house and bet my heart

On what reminds me of my love.
I know that's going to mean enough.
The gods of form and fortune know

I will not lose. Now off they go.

The Furthest West

You lot got dazzled and burned
All afternoon. We two were last to arrive,
Tipsy and hand in hand
And, if they go, and they do, will be last to leave.

The rocks encroach and the Cornish sand stretches
Where we settle. This
Is the furthest west she says she has gone for ages,
Which isn't true, I think, but I say yes.

Blues emerge and blur, like the promenade sketcher
Couldn't do edges well and thought
A vague, dark and watery picture
The pricier art.

Fine constellations spoil his plan. I
Sweep them up in my right hand.
More grains in here, you know, than stars in the sky.
Yes, she says with a sniff. Other way round.

Now the sea goes quiet, straining to hear
Our shared and differing views.
Then gathers, rolling, breaking clean out of nowhere
Its only news.

Watching Over

Elated by ourselves, we shift and slip –
Mouths open with the memory of a kiss –
Parting in two to sleep, and if it's mine

Then that was it, that break above, and now
It's yours I wake to witness your unknowing
Our love and all you know.
                              Some ancient will,
Though night is safe and quiet here, commands
You be watched over now, and, to that end,
Exacerbates the wind and whipping rains,
Or amplifies the howls of animals
To make my waking watchful and tense,
Though for a thousand miles there is no mind
To hurt you, nor one raindrop on the wind.

Lust

Lust is at home here and I make it welcome.
I offer it stuff it accepts but would otherwise take.
    Beautiful telling ache.
Lust will be last to leave this all-nite affair,
    Make no mistake,
    And it was welcome,
    But I live here.

Conquest

His house, his town, his garden, his own room
Sprout with memory, jungle-green and seething.
He was a Spaniard, gilded and immune.
Now he's a native, sickly and just breathing.

The Sentence

Lied to like a judge I stepped down.
My court cleared to the shrieks of the set free.
I know the truth, I know its level sound.
It didn't speak, or didn't speak to me.

The jury caught the tan of her bright look,
The ushers smoothed her path and bowed aside,
The lawyers watched her fingers as she took
Three solemn vows, her lipstick as she lied.

She vowed and lied to me and won her case.
I'm glad she won. I wouldn't have had her led
However gently into the shrunken space
I'd opened for her. There. There now it's said,

Said in this chamber where I sleep of old,
Alone with books and sprawling robes and scent.
With all I have, I have no power to hold
The innocent or the found innocent.

The Night Is Young

I was with some friends when I noticed with some strangers
One of the Gang. And we rose like we'd won awards,
Reluctant and delighted, to a position
Halfway between our tables, and began,
Began with a tale of now and ourselves, but soon
Were hurrying back in the years like children yelled
Out of the light of their inexplicable game,
Into the brooding houses to be held.

Nothing's changed, we said, since everything had.
Again some time, we agreed, as it never would.
When I sipped and caught him searching my eyes for the kind
I was, he caught me searching his for the same.

Though my new friends and his, from time to time,
Would look across and point out a seat in the ring
For either stranger, no, we remained right there,
Steadily finishing off what was there to be said,
Drinking and putting our tankards down slowly.

And when there was nothing listing the names like somehow
They'd be around us, the Gang, like the night there was no one
Missing. Weren't we over there by the window?

I'd seen some, but he'd seen two I expected
Never to see again, they were fine, they were fine,
He mentioned, and that was that.
                              I returned to my circle,
Shaking him off as doubtless he shook me off,
Answering who he was with an oh someone,
Settling to the night, uncomfortable, gruff,
And feeling about as young as the night is young,
And wanting it all, like one who has had enough.
You don't forgive what's left of what you loved.

If You Haven't Got a Shilling

Christmas came so fast around the corner
We concluded we were lost or perhaps had taken
A misdirection when we'd stopped and spoken
Thankfully to the kindliest-looking stranger.
Perhaps we'd been too thankful to be listening.

Our youngest throat had barely healed from singing,
Our oldest eye from a twinkle. Certain of us
Had said goodbye for good and all to Christmas,
But there nevertheless he was, planting and grinning.
I did hear shouts behind us: 'What's the hold-up?'

As we bumped into each other as we pulled up.
Neighbour and neighbour nudged and were crying 'Humbug!'
Or saying 'I'm Dutch if it is!' then 'Eat your homburg!'
When clearly it was. So kids were heaved and held up
To stare comprehendingly at the hinting visage.

We sat down gladly, chuckling back the message,
Greeted with some hysteria, some corpsing,
Indubitably some embarrassment at his timing,
But largely with goodwill. After all, the passage
Is not his fault, his business, or our business.

'Well, if he says so, fine!' was the consensus.
We'll do our bit, we always have, we want to!
We told him we all wondered where he went to
Every year, which brought a tear to Christmas,
Because he really thinks we do all wonder.

Curse on a Child

*Darlin', think of me as a stopping train. I go all
the way, but you can get off anywhere you like.*
MALE ADVANCE, OVERHEARD

May the love of your life get on at Ongar
        And wake up sleeping on Terminal 4.
May his anorak grow big with jotters
        Noting the numbers of trains he saw.
May he read these out in a reedy voice,
        May he drink real ale with his mates while you
Blink in the smoke. May his hair be a joke.
        May his happiest hour have been spent in Crewe.

May he call for you in a lime-green van,
        May his innermost thoughts be anyone's guess.
May his answer to 'Who's your favourite band?'
        Be the only occasion he answers 'YES,'
But then may he add, 'When Wakeman was with 'em,'
        And play you the evidence. May what he wears
Never again be in vogue. May his mother
        Dote, devote, and move in downstairs.

May your French turn frog, may your croissant go straight,
        May your bread be Hovis, your wine home-made,
May your spice be Old Spice, your only lingerie
        Les fronts-igrec, and your beauty fade.
May you curl in the Land of Nod like the child
        You were when you wouldn't, and screamed all the way
From Perpignan to the Gare de Lyon,
        Echoed through Paris, and on to Calais.

The man in the corner, who sat with his head
        Awake in his hands, has issued this curse.
He is far away now. What keeps him awake
        Isn't screaming, or crying, or writing verse.
It is sometimes nothing but quiet, sloping,
        My terrible infant, looming and deep.
May you never know it. May your life be as boring
        As men can make it, but, dear, may you sleep.

Don't Waste Your Breath

On sales or sermons at my door,
Contributions from the floor,
    Screaming things.
Wondering where the good times went,
Complaining to this Government,
    Reciting 'Kings'.

Telling fibs to Sherlock Holmes,
Games of tag with garden gnomes,
    Soliloquies.
Knock-knock jokes on a Croatian,
Great ideas for situation
    Comedies.

Asking her to reconsider
Leaving, trying to kid a kidder,
    Roundelays.
Entering for field events,
Just causes or impediments
    On wedding days.

Begging rides in backs of hearses,
Happy Birthday's other verses,
    Asking twice.
Musing on your point-blank misses,
Moaning 'This is hell' or 'This is
    Paradise.'

Offering a monk your ticket,
Using metaphors from cricket
    When in Texas.
Telephoning during finals,
Remonstrating in urinals
    With your Exes.

Phrases like 'Here's what I think',
Giving up girls/smoking/drink
    At New Year.
Asserting that all men are equal,
Settling down to write a sequel
    To *King Lear*.

Revisions to *The Odyssey*,
Improvements on Psalm 23
    Or hazel eyes.
Glueing back the arms on Venus,
Any other rhyme than 'penis',
    The Turner Prize.

Interrogating diplomats,
Defining Liberal Democrats,
    Begging to banks.
Supporting Malta's football team,
Translating King's 'I have a dream'
    Into the Manx.

Reading verse to lesser mammals,
Tailing cats or humping camels,
    Hectoring sheep.
Pleading with a traffic warden,
Writing things that sound like Auden
    In his sleep.

Don't waste your breath on telling me
My purpose, point or pedigree
    Or wit or worth.
Don't waste your breath explaining how
A poem works, or should do now
    You're on the Earth.

Don't waste your breath on rage, regret
Or ridicule; don't force or fret,
    Breathe easily.
Remember: every starlit suck
Is seven trillion parts good luck
    To one part me.

Museum

Sundays, like a stanza break
    Or shower's end of all applause,
For some old unexplaining sake
    The optimistic tread these shores,
As lonely as the dead awake
    Or God among the dinosaurs.

Sulk

What we are at is pining for our lost
    Future. How we are doing that is simple:
Slouching beside our low glass tables dressed
    In shimmering precious suit from nape to ankle.

That's how it was to have been. The walls of silver,
    The doors that slish behind, the ultramarine
Drink, the apotheosis of the letter
    Z in Christian names and the light this clean.

Instead it's a sulk we'll have. We're the spoiled child
    With centuries for uncles, and those uncles
Leaning along the shelves disabused and old
    And letting us learn or not from the foul troubles

They dumped on us. Well we're not going to bother.
    We're going to sit here in our suits and shine,
Move and amend and move and adjourn forever,
    And pour the green olorosos of the moon,

Aren't we, Zardoq, though till the yawn of Time
    The rough and the brown and sick make war and changes
Backwards into the country, into the storm,
    And cluster there by the millpond of the ages.

The Margit-Isle
(for Patrick Howarth)

The boy had died. We knew that right away.
'Es gibt kein Luft,' I said. On a cold day
We should have seen his breath as a cone of mist.
I was proud I'd used some German words. We stood
In a park in Budapest.

        Some passers-by
Did just that with a glance. The German fat guy
Peered and shrugged and went. A flashy rich
Prostitute arrived. She was the first
And only one to touch.

        It was 2 pm.
Nothing happened. 'The police are going to come,
And we've no papers,' I fretted. Patrick said:
'They won't ask anything,' and an ambulance
Braked and no one did.

        They hauled him up.
His anorak hood fell back. Our little group
Saw now he was a girl. She could have died
Of drugs or cold, stabwound or rope or rape.
Least bad was suicide.

        They drove away.
We'll never know a thing. We spent the day
In the tight conspiracy of private shocks.
A clerk in police HQ would make some notes
And slide them in a box.

        A year and a half
And I'd do this, predictably enough.
In Hungary perhaps they shed some light
On why she died, but light shed on a death
Is not what I call light.

I was waiting.
To bring some writer's thinking to the writing.
Of what it was to chance on the fresh dead
In public in broad daylight in the middle
Of where we are. Instead

It's ended up as dry as a lucky stone.
Something to carry around and feel. Move on.

The Great Detectives

None can leap as far as the great detectives.
Not only can they bare the cause as if
It stripped itself in public, they can sniff
Effects it never had till now, or motives
Stuffed in coats, contemptibly denied
By those who did it, know it, and can't hide.

None can sleep as light as the great sleuths.
To them the stars are evidence, the moon
A gaping witness and the nightmares soon
Resolved into incriminating truths.
The corn of life is twisted into scenes.
Who have the time and reason have the means.

Who hangs about that drawing-room alone?
None now, where failures trot to the great chair
And ring around its ankles like a fair.
Then everything is epilogue, is known.
After the accusation's shot and stuck,
Who's left will make an innocence of luck.

No certainties like those of private eyes,
Once the detecting bug is coughed and caught:
Whatever art is made, or history taught,
What isn't Law might just as well be lies
For all the help it brings in the hot nights
Before the white steam clears and he alights.

No charm like his, no eccentricities
So crisp, authenticating and sincere.
And, as for her, who would have thought it here?
That she could solve so many with such ease?
But better turn those hooks and curious eyes
To joyful exclamations of surprise!

The truth is out with murder and with blood.
They drape across the sofas of the town.
Whatever may be used is taken down.
A friend runs into strangers in a wood.
He shrugs the shoulders that the earth has picked
To flop upon and sleep. In the next act

The corpse is quiet. Once the avenging eyes
Have gone out for each other and for good,
The guiltlessness will swell like a flash flood
And thunder as it must, where the land lies
Low and weak, then crack out to the sea
That mutters Hamlet's question endlessly.

The great detectives of our time we'll never
See at first hand, ours is a later book.
We don't know how it ends though we do look,
Climb nervously ahead to the dust cover
And peer at names. We can't expect the murder.
We must be those who don't. We're not the reader:

We have to cast about this ancient pile
Without a host, and make our plans together;
Or sleep alone and dream of one another,
And pause in all its chambers for a while,
Lift every implement, have every cause,
Be watched in silence through the double doors.

We have to know we could appear to be
Accomplice, alibi or, munching there,
The thirteenth guest who's welcome to his chair,
For how we need him in our company.
But, when the porch is darkened with the shape
Of hat and stick, of case and folded cape,

When all are drawn towards him in a room,
As shadows of suspicion fall like cards,
When some are lost and some are lost for words,
And some, forgetting, gratefully assume –
Be out of that dead chapter like the clues
He couldn't understand, so wouldn't use.

The Devil at War

That truce didn't last.
    The dark school dropped its people on to the road
Like dice cast
    Loudly on a classroom desk lid
Just
    As silence starts. *Who did that?* Well, he did.

We pull away to the hills, from where we see
    Thunder, dawn, or sheer
Emptiness unbolt the clouds, as the thing on high
    Has its one idea:
Catastrophe
    Somewhere or here.

The Devil bikes around, helping. He does!
    The Devil is not powerful. He cannot
Die. He steps on a mine, he stubs his toes.
    Like hell they hurt
But he bikes on. He goes
    To a gunman *Have a heart!*

He tries
    To free some hostages. He throws his arm
Round homesick Irish, Spanish, Canadian UN guys
    Who wake up in alarm
Alone, in the cold sunrise.
    He does no harm.

He is spotted moving across
    A no-man's-land while corporals scream *Go back!*
And bullets criss-cross
    His mending heart, which can only ache
Or endure loss,
    And is black.

We lose the Devil
       During a siege, but he crops up now in a newsreel
Trying with a Red Cross man to heave some rubble
       Off a shop girl,
But unable,
       And unhopeful.

The Devil we freeze in a frame
       Is stepping back, too tired,
Hands on his head. The Devil is doing the same
       Every day, while the Lord
Locks the gates of a camp, apportions blame,
       Gives His Word.

The Altered Slightly

Hilarious to the virus that has spent
its infinite resources
concocting itself anew,

these healers, helicoptered into a war zone,
with helmets and a peace plan,
pound the maps in a shell of an HQ.

Under the microscope the enemies goggle
in yellow and red grease,
their tricorn shapes a shock, and somebody says

*That's them but if you look
they've altered slightly*. Good news for the sniper,
who sights the Muslim wandering up the road,

then sights the Christian limping in the gutter,
and cannot choose between them or to let them
come and have each other. The dead,

uniquely in the dark about who did it,
lie still as stone, mistaken for the hiding,
while somewhere in some dedicated rich

lab the virgin germs,
nervous in molecular pitch dark,
parachute into a slide of blood

and set to work.

Yellow Plates

The family moving into the house were told
    To make themselves at home.

But dropping their things in a heap in the bare centre
    Of the largest, warmest room,

They had wondered how in hell they could cook a meal
    For twelve in a strange kitchen

(What with the brothers so drunk on the national drink
    And the grandchildren

Wailing the infant anthems *Why is nobody*
    Looking at me alone

Or *Take the others away until I need them*
    Or *What's undone's undone*)

But they found the cooking terribly easy, for here
    Was a fridge, a working oven

With even a clock, and here was a pile of matching
    Yellow plates: five, six, seven.

The Sarajevo Zoo

Men had used up their hands, men had
offered, cupped, or kissed them to survive,
had wiped them on the skirts of their own town,
as different men had shinned up a ladder and taken
    the sun down.

One man had upped his arms in a victory U
to a thousand others, to show how much of the past
he did not know and would not know when he died.
Another's joke was the last a hostage heard:
    Oh I lied

which did win some applause from the bare hands
of dozing men. And others of course had never
fired before, then fired, for the work of hands
was wild and sudden in those days
    in those lands.

For men. For the women there was
the stroke, the ripping of hair, the smearing of tears,
snot, and there was the prod of a shaking man,
or with fused palms the gibbering prayer
    to the U.N.

The nothing they had between those palms was
hope and the yard between surrendering palms
was hope as well. Far off, a fist in the sky
was meaning hope but if you prised it open
    you saw why.

The hands of the children here were wringing themselves
hot with the plight of animals over there,
and drawing them in their pens with the crimson rain
of what men do to each other on television
    crayoned in.

But hands continued to feed the demented bear
who ate two other bears to become the last
bear in the Sarajevo Zoo. And they fed him
when they could, two Bosnian zookeepers
        all autumn.

Today I read that that time ended too,
when fifteen rifles occupying some thirty
hands got there and crept in a rank on knees
towards the smoke of the blown and stinking cages
        and black trees.

Trees were what you could not see the starving
beasts behind, or see there were now no beasts,
only the keepers crouching with their two lives.
Then winter howled a command and the sorry branches
        shed their leaves.

A Force That Ate Itself

They had marched on crust an infinitude of miles
    Eleven abreast. Just
Pages and pages of mud to read on the heels
    Of the one in front. They went
    As far as the eye could see, as far
        As the eye could bear.

Life in the force was hard and special, the time
    Empty of women. Someone
Tried aloud to remember them, but the same
    Silence fell like a quill
    Responding to a plea for love
        In the negative.

Gone were the crowd and gone were the enemy
    Months ago. There was no
Danger at hand or ahead, no charge or mêlée,
    No line to cross or cross
    To hold aloft, or peace to keep,
        Or war to stop;

Only the march of the only army there was,
    Eleven abreast. Just
Trudging the world in a line to endless applause
    From the last god, Mud,
    The Caliban in love below
        Who won't let go.

They trod the world so small the men they found
    Up ahead, quite mad,
Were their own tail but they cut them to the ground
    In innocence, and once
    Begun it could not be stopped, not until
        Each General

Had shot himself from behind and shuffled on.
This, luckily, would be
Impossible on our Earth, where no man
Can catch himself himself,
But some can tear each other in half
So don't laugh

At a world that had forgotten it was round.
Now it's a small brown ball,
And the muck of its surface thinks with a giggled sound
Of the weight of men, of a time when
War went briskly through the crops
With high hopes.

The People's Cinema

As blank as scripture to a ruling class
Discussed in hells they do not think exist,
Cracked and abandoned to the slicing grass
    And disabusing dust,
A movie screen shows nothing in a morning mist.

Here's where the happy endings were never had,
Or, like the long and lonely, never shown.
No one rode to the rescue of who was good,
    No star was born, none shone,
No dream came true, or fun began, or life went on.

A Classical outside. Like a parthenon
Or meant to be, but more as if that mother
Had quite disowned this worn and woebegone
    Shell of light. Its father
Was a woman's face in a glass. She ordered it like weather.

Here's where the stepping leg of a pale princess
Would never gleam in the flank of a silver Merc,
No carpet lap at the tips of an angel's dress
    As that began its catwalk,
No head be turned or heart won, none have all the luck.

It had to open faster than today.
She scratched a deadline on the skin of earth.
They couldn't meet it but they couldn't say.
    They swallowed back their breath.
The sun abruptly set in each unchewing mouth.

Here's where the plans were laid, and here ignored,
Here they were changed, here lied about, here lost,
Here's where they pulled the trick they could afford,
    Here's where they paid the cost,
Where a workman sang all day, baked in a wall to the waist,

When every short cut snapped on the one night,
Caving and bulging floors like a bigger child
Had waded from the future for a fight,
    And each thing was spilled,
Each dimly praying gap of air was found and filled.

The light went out on no one knows how few:
Interred, incinerated, a foot stuck out
Live from a ceiling waving in a shoe
    As the auditorium set,
And the sun was down, and the building up, and the deadline met,

And no one goes there now except to nod.
At what you get when men take on the sun.
At what men do when told to by a god
    Who's gone, and wasn't one.
How riches look in daylight when there *are* none.

The Allies

Us? We were with the Allies. We were with you
Right on the dot, throughout, and we were with you
At and beyond the end. We were with the Allies.

And when we were with you we felt we were something more
Than a nation, we were a brotherhood, a cause.
Nobody said we flouted or broke things.

The enemy had one eye, though, that was simple.
It's hard to know what's right till the night you know
What wrong is and the enemy was what wrong is.

You great big nations thought of us and said 'Them?
They're with the Allies.' So we got added to prayers.
The name of our land was mouthed before the Amen

By your fair little children. In their schools
They crayoned us in like everyone, in the colour
The Allies were, and did projects on our products.

They told their mothers the things we make, but their mothers
Showed them them in tins. They had bought our products
Because we were allies. We were the Allies' allies.

After, we made our way to the capitals
Of superpowers, observed by the delicate ladies
Who live in them, and one told another one 'Them?

They were with us,' and that was like having new friends
Always passing, too well-bred to wave back.
Stroll by the Jubilee Arch as the sun goes down:

Ours are the curious names on the marble walls
As high as the eye can see. You have to remember
Our language has no vowels but it can be mastered.

Oh yes, we were with the Allies. Me myself?
I'll tell you about my war and about my wife
And daughters too if this fellow will ever serve me.

The Horses' Mouths

FROM *Phaeton and the Chariot of the Sun*

I *Pyrois*

Film me in silhouette. I insist. I'm not
Them prancing nags. Is that thing rolling? No?
Good. It better not be. What you got,
Rothmans? Gimme. What do you want to know?

The boy. The boy in the chariot? Oh no.
Some things I crack about, some things I don't.
You learn the worst is never long ago.
We horses live our lives in the word *won't*

But you don't understand, you undergods.
Gimme the Bushmills. Woh, that hits the spot.
The boy in the chariot. Hell. It makes no odds.
It happened. Why? This isn't lit. Why not?

What was the story... Somebody made him think
His father wasn't his father? Right, so he snaps
And goes and gets his way. Dies in the drink.
Talking of which... No, you pedalling chaps

Think you're as free as air though you're made of earth.
You got to obey your whim like a whipped horse
Flies. That boy. He thought about his birth.
He wanted it again. He ran his course.

How did you find me here?
> This is my refuge from all human voices,
> Their differences that shrivel into hisses
All indistinct, their faces
> Merged to the infinite grains of a far shore

Licked by the dog sea.
> Here on my noiseless meadow I ride alone,
> Ride, ride myself with the wind on my spine,
While the fuelled and roaring Sun
> Mislays my name in the mess of his tyranny.

Talk to the others, friend.
> Find the unkempt Pyrois; Aethon, vain
> And cosseted by Man, then look for Phlegon
Anywhere where the thin
> Are all there is, and the wind is a hurled sand.

That's his gesture. Mine?
> Mine's this solitude. I've a world to tell
> But not this world. We switched your sky into Hell
And all for a human will,
> Its pride, its point, its prick. It will come again.

How did I know it was him?
> When we were torn through clouds and the East Wind
> I felt no weight on my back, heard no command,
And felt no pull, no hand,
> No pilot. No escape now. Kingdom come.

Three images, that's all.
> One was his face, the boy, his face when he lost
> The reins and then his footing – that was the last
We saw of him – he must
> Presumably have gone in a fireball –

Another was how the Moon,
> Seeing us hurtle by, reminded us all
> Of the face of a mother beside a carousel,
Worrying herself ill,
> As her children wave, are gone, are back too soon –

And another was afterwards.
    I lay for a good forever somewhere in a woods.
    The petrified seconds prayed, the hours wore hoods.
'You gods,' I said, 'you gods.'
    And those, I trusted, those were my final words

To men. Instead, these are:
    Forget Eous, leave me alone in my meadow,
    Riding myself, racing my sisterly shadow
Into the shade, where sorrow
    Wraps her and deserts me, drenched, here.

III *Aethon*

One minute, love.
You're looking at
The winner of
The 2.15,
3.38
And 5 o'clock.
I haven't time.
I race, I work.

Ask what you want
But ask it fast.
The time you spend
Is time I lose,
Is time we've lost.
Aethon never
Loses, friend,
You got that? Ever.

The chariot?
The idiot boy?
I don't admit
And never shall
I lost that day.
He may have done.
He burned. So what?
His father's son.

157

The countries burned,
The oceans steamed,
The stinking wind
It filled my eyes.
I never dreamed
Years afterwards
I'd humble all
These thoroughbreds

Day in day out,
Year after year,
Beyond all doubt
Beyond compare,
The sight they fear,
Aethon, pride
Of any course
You humans ride.

If all the gold
That lights this room
Was melted, rolled
And stretched for me,
I should in time
Reach Heaven's Gate
And there I'd not
Be made to wait

But rode by servants
Back to where
I rode the Heavens
Once, the Sun
Would part the air
For Aethon,
Fanfared, forgiven
Aethon.

IV *Phlegon*

Get on my back. You all do in the end.
You've come some way to go the way you came,
  But shall do, all the same,
  My doubly hopping friend,
At least you ride in peace, at least you ask my name.

Where are the other three? There's no surprise.
Eous rippling aimlessly alone,
  Pyrois wrecked, Aethon?
  Neighing at blue skies,
As if his loss, our loss, was some grand race he'd won.

I work this zone. Don't have to, but I do.
I do have to, and so would you. Look now,
  The planters on the brow,
  They falter, wondering who
Wants what of them and why. They'll try to question you.

Be plain with them. It waters you with hope
That in this desert where the fire can't die
  Nor air reach to the sky,
  Somehow they grow a crop
That doesn't care it's dead, that doesn't know. Now stop,

Get off my back. Feel hotness on each sole
And howl. For this is not the word made flesh,
  This is the word made ash,
  This is the mouth made hole,
Here where the star fell, here where he got his wish.

Stargazing

The night is fine and dry. It falls and spreads
the cold sky with a million opposites
that, for a moment, seem like a million souls
and soon, none, and then, for what seems a long time,
one. Then of course it spins. What is better to do
than string out over the infinite dead spaces
the ancient beasts and spearmen of the human
mind, and, if not the real ones, new ones?

But, try making them clear to one you love –
whoever is standing by you is one you love
when pinioned by the stars – you will find it quite
impossible, but like her more for thinking
she sees that constellation.

After the wave of pain, you will turn to her
and, in an instant, change the universe
to a sky you were glad you came outside to see.

This is the act of all the descended gods
of every age and creed: to weary of all
that never ends, to take a human hand,
and go back into the house.